Presented to

Chloe

From

Mimi

On this date

Christmas
2021

Daily Prayers for a Girl's Heart

BARBOUR **kidz**

A Division of Barbour Publishing

© 2014 by Barbour Publishing, Inc.

ISBN 978-1-64352-442-9

Published by Barbour Publishing, Inc., 1810 Barbour Drive, Uhrichsville, Ohio 44683, www.barbourbooks.com

Our mission is to inspire the world with the life-changing message of the Bible.

Printed in China.

000670 0521 HA

Day 1
Your Plan for My Life

Dear God, I spend a lot of time thinking about the future and wondering what my life will look like. Right now it's pretty basic: I go to school, I spend time with my friends and family, and a bunch of extracurricular and church activities take up the rest of my time. But I wonder what happens when I'm done with school and I no longer live with my family—what will my life look like then? The Bible says that You have a plan for each of us. Help me to trust Your will and Your plan for my life. You already know what I will do in the next fifty years, even though I have no idea. That's so crazy to think about! Thank You for the plans that You have in store for me. Help me to trust Your words and to listen for Your voice when I'm making big decisions. Amen.

For you created my inmost being;
you knit me together in my mother's womb.
PSALM 139:13 NIV

Day 2
Staying in Bed

Lord, some days I just want to stay in bed and pull the covers over my head. I don't want to be with people because people can be mean and hurtful and scary. They hurt my feelings or make me mad. If I stay here in this safe place, I won't have to worry about how others treat me.

I wonder if my friends ever feel this way, Lord. Wow. I wonder if my mom and dad ever feel this way. I hope I never do or say anything to make them afraid to get out of bed.

All I really want is to be loved and accepted. I want people to think I'm fun and cool and worth spending time with. I want people to like me, Lord. And the more I think about it, I guess that's what everybody wants.

Help me love others the way I want to be loved. Help me to make every person I come in contact with feel good about herself. I want to be the kind of friend, sister, and daughter who makes people want to get out of bed. . .not stay in it and hide. Amen.

"My command is this:
Love each other as I have loved you."
JOHN 15:12 NIV

Day 3
A Forever Home

Dear God, heaven must be an awesome place. I've heard about it all my life, especially when people die. I know that people don't just go in the ground; they live somewhere forever. Some people say that everyone goes to heaven, but the Bible tells me that only those who know You and have their sins forgiven will be there.

Help me remember that eternity is more important than this world. I don't know how long my life will last here, but eternity doesn't end. That's really hard for me to think about! I mean, imagine never dying! It will be totally wonderful to spend forever with You in that amazing place!

I want my friends and family to be there with me, God. Show me how to tell them about You so they can be ready to meet You someday.

Thank You for being with me through all my life and for giving me an eternal home in heaven. I love You. Amen.

♥

"There is more than enough room in my Father's home. If this were not so, would I have told you that I am going to prepare a place for you? When everything is ready, I will come and get you, so that you will always be with me where I am."
JOHN 14:2–3 NLT

Day 4
Plans for Tomorrow

Lord, as I lie here in bed, I'm thinking about the plans I have for tomorrow. I know how I would like things to go but am worried about what will happen. Will I pass the test in school? Will I make it on the soccer team? Will I embarrass myself in gym? Will the teacher accept the project I've been working so hard to finish? Will my parents be pleased with my next report card?

There are so many things on my mind, I'm finding it hard to settle down to sleep. But one thing I do know is that no matter where I am or what I am doing, You are watching over me. You are looking out for me no matter what challenges I face.

Thank You for blessing my life, for making sure I have enough of everything I need. Thank You for guiding me when I am not sure what I should do and for protecting me. With You in my life, I need not fear anything.

So I now close my eyes, knowing that You will keep me safe while I sleep and that I will wake up to a new day of new possibilities with You by my side.

The Lord is my Shepherd [to feed,
guide, and shield me], I shall not lack.
PSALM 23:1 AMPC

Day 5
The Beauty of the Heart

Heavenly Father, Your Word says that You look at our hearts to determine our beauty. It is much more important who I am on the inside than what I look like on the outside. I have to admit, though, that it is easy to get caught up in fashion and makeup. The world around me seems to say that I need those things in order to be pretty.

I want to be a girl who honors You in every aspect of my life, including the choices I make regarding how I dress and present myself. Help me be aware as I begin to grow up that the clothes I wear and the amount of makeup on my face send a message to those around me. I ask You to give me confidence in who I am as Your daughter. Help me to believe that I am beautiful just as You made me and that I do not need to add a lot of "extras" to my appearance.

Your beauty should not come from outward adornment, such as elaborate hairstyles and the wearing of gold jewelry or fine clothes. Rather, it should be that of your inner self, the unfading beauty of a gentle and quiet spirit, which is of great worth in God's sight.
1 PETER 3:3–4 NIV

Day 6
Nowhere to Run

God, You know *everything* about me? That's a scary thought! But when I consider that You know and yet still love me—that wraps around me like a warm blanket. I don't have to pretend anything with You (You already know anyway!). It's wonderful to have a Friend who can understand me better than I understand myself.

Even when I want to hide from You, I can't. Psalm 139 says that You know everything I have done, am doing, and will do. Nothing is hidden from You. You go before me, follow after, and lead and protect me every step of my life.

I feel like the psalmist when he says, "Such knowledge is too wonderful for me, too great for me to understand!" (Psalm 139:6 NLT). Even if I tried, I couldn't get away from You! You would run right after me. There is nowhere I can go to get away from Your presence. Ever. A love so deep and strong is impossible for me to grasp. Help remind me of that, Lord, when I am filled with doubts about being loved. Amen.

O LORD, you have examined my heart
and know everything about me. You know
when I sit down or stand up. You know
my thoughts even when I'm far away.
PSALM 139:1–2 NLT

Day 7
A Good Model

Father, I pray that You would provide good role models for me throughout my lifetime. Please give me wisdom about who I look up to as I get older. Help me to be careful about who I trust and who I allow into my heart. Your Word tells me to guard my heart (Proverbs 4:23) and also that Your peace will protect my heart as I follow Jesus (Philippians 4:7). Thank You for those wise words of wisdom!

Help me to understand that not everyone who claims to be a Christian has a true relationship with You. I pray You would give me the ability to understand right from wrong and to be able to tell when someone is true or fake.

The Bible is Your Word to us, and I believe it is alive and active (Hebrews 4:12)! Your Word is the bottom line—the source of truth. Please let the role models in my life live by it and always point me toward the truth. Help me to remember that anytime I'm confused by what someone says about You, I can turn to Your Word for the truth. Amen.

Join together in following my example, brothers and sisters, and just as you have us as a model, keep your eyes on those who live as we do.
PHILIPPIANS 3:17 NIV

Day 8
Thoughts

Lord, I know thoughts can be very powerful. I've heard it said, "You are what you eat." So it only makes sense that you are what you think. In fact, the Bible tells me that!

And it all comes down to the heart, doesn't it? What I truly think and believe is how I will be. If I set my thoughts on things that are sad, I will be sad. If I think about good things, I will feel good. This seems to be a rule that can be applied to any situation.

So, Lord, help me keep a positive attitude. Help me to think of good things. Plant Your Word in me so that I will keep in mind all the things You say are important—loving others (even enemies), obeying my parents, being kind to everyone, forgiving people (including myself), taking care of my body, and being content in every situation. Help me to make Your Word my word, in all I do and say. Build me up within to look on the bright side no matter what is happening on the outside. Each day give me a new heart and mind focused on Your Light. Amen.

For as he thinks in his heart, so is he.
PROVERBS 23:7 NKJV

Day 9
Your Instruction Book

Sometimes I wish I had an instruction manual for my life, Lord, but then I realize You've already taken care of that. You've given us Your Word to guide us through this journey of life. I'm sorry that I don't always treat it with the value it deserves—it can lie beside my bed, unopened, as I try to find my way through life on my own. But You have had Your words written down so that I can learn from the mistakes of people who have messed up, as well as learn from the good choices others have made in doing things Your way. I can read about how much You love me, how You forgive me, and what I need to do to act and live wisely.

God, thank You for not expecting me to try to figure things out on my own. You have given me Your Word so that I can grow closer to You. Thank You for sharing Your "instruction manual" with me! Amen.

All Scripture is inspired by God and is useful to teach us what is true and to make us realize what is wrong in our lives. It corrects us when we are wrong and teaches us to do what is right.
2 TIMOTHY 3:16 NLT

Day 10
Forgiving Myself

Dear God, I get so frustrated with myself sometimes when I mess up and don't do things perfectly. Like when I get mad at my mom over a tiny issue, or don't hand in my homework on time because I got distracted by my friends or a really good book. I know that I can never do things perfectly, but I still have that desire in my heart. When I see how far I really am from perfect, it sometimes makes me feel hopeless, like there's no point in even trying to be good. When I start thinking this way, help me to remember that You didn't create me to be perfect and that what I do has no influence over how much You love me. There is nothing that I could do to earn Your love, and I thank You for that gift. Help me to extend the same grace to myself that You do, that I would be able to forgive myself for not being perfect and remember the forgiveness You have given me. Amen.

If you kept record of our sins, no one could last long. But you forgive us, and so we will worship you.
Psalm 130:3–4 CEV

Day 11
The Gift of Friendship

Dear God, thank You for the friends that You have given me. I am so thankful for each girl in my life, and I pray that You would continue to bless all of my friendships. Sometimes it's hard to be a good friend; it's easier to be selfish and concentrate on what makes me happy or what I want to do. Help me to remember to put others first and to settle any disagreements with kindness and gentleness. Show me how to serve my friends, whether it's listening to them vent when they've had a really bad day or surprising them with their favorite candy bar. I want to be a good friend and show them how much I care. Also, help me not to show favoritism and to love each friend individually. Sometimes I connect more with one friend than another. When that happens, help me to show them love equally. Thank You for being the perfect example of a friend who loves at all times. Amen.

But the wisdom from above is first of all pure.
It is also peace loving, gentle at all times,
and willing to yield to others. It is full of mercy
and the fruit of good deeds. It shows no
favoritism and is always sincere.
JAMES 3:17 NLT

Day 12
Controlling My Anger

Oh, people can get me so angry, Lord! It starts as a small feeling, but it's like a fire, soon spreading all through me. It takes over my brain so that I can think of nothing but the injustice that was done to me. I can't understand how someone could treat me like that, and I rage inside.

I read in Your Word that You were angry once, in the temple, when people were turning Your meeting place into a store of sorts. What was to be a holy place was filled with those trying to make some money. I get angry when I feel used too!

But I can learn from Your example, Jesus. You were angry but didn't let it lead to sin. You dealt with the problem and moved on. It didn't turn into bitterness and rage.

I know I shouldn't let my anger get out of control, Father. Please help me to keep it in check so that it doesn't develop into hostility.

Understand this, my dear brothers and sisters:
You must all be quick to listen, slow to speak,
and slow to get angry. Human anger does not
produce the righteousness God desires.
JAMES 1:19–20 NLT

Day 13
Saved by a Gift

Dear Father, I have to thank You for the plan of salvation. The Bible says that everyone living on earth is a sinner; we are all far from You. But You didn't want us to be lost forever and sent Your Son to pay for our sins.

I know what sin is. I have done many things wrong, maybe not like killing somebody or stealing a car or robbing a bank, but I've told lies and disobeyed my parents and said unkind things. I've felt what guilt is like; I know that dirty feeling inside.

That's why I'm glad Jesus is my Savior. Thank You for dying on the Cross and making a way for me to be in a personal relationship with You. Thank You for taking my guilt upon Yourself and giving me a clean heart. Thank You for going through pain so that I can know Your love and forgiveness.

I have friends who don't know about this good news, Lord. Help me to be a witness, a light shining out for You. I want to tell others about this great gift. Amen.

For the wages of sin is death, but the gift of God is eternal life in Christ Jesus our Lord.
ROMANS 6:23 NKJV

Day 14
A Way Out

Every day, Lord, I face a ton of temptations. Sometimes I have an overwhelming urge to get another new outfit, a fabulous pair of shoes, or boxes and boxes of chocolate. Then at other times I am tempted in a different way, such as wanting to text late at night when I'm supposed to be sleeping.

All these temptations could get really aggravating if I didn't realize I have a few great things in my favor. One is the fact that I'm not alone. Lots of people are tempted. So it's good to know I'm normal. Another is that You, God, have promised to help me be strong—and will show me a way out! I need not feel trapped, but need to merely look for whatever exit You've provided. But best of all is the fact that if I do cave, You will not only forgive me but help me be stronger the next time.

So thank You, Lord, for being greater than any temptation I may face. Amen.

The temptations in your life are no different from what others experience. And God is faithful. He will not allow the temptation to be more than you can stand. When you are tempted, he will show you a way out so that you can endure.
1 CORINTHIANS 10:13 NLT

Day 15
Being Content with Ordinary

I wish I could be content with being average, God, but it's hard when the magazines and the commercials say you shouldn't be. On the TV shows, the average people are the dumpy ones, the ones everybody has a laugh at. They provide the humor; they're not the heroes. The average girls are the good friends of the main character, but they don't get the Cinderella ending.

I guess I should be encouraged when I think about all the average people I've heard about in the Bible. Many of them were just ordinary people doing ordinary things, and yet You used them. David was a shepherd boy, and Mary was a small-town girl. But You knew their names, and You had a place for them. Help me remember that You have a place for me as well. And give me the wisdom not to base my idea of significance on TV-show characters. Amen.

"For I know the plans I have for you," declares the LORD, "plans to prosper you and not to harm you, plans to give you hope and a future."
JEREMIAH 29:11 NIV

Day 16
Just Bein' Me

Lord, why is it so hard not to want to be someone else? Everywhere I look there is someone with "more" than what I have. They are more popular, prettier, have more money, a better family, more friends, more opportunities. The list seems endless. The problem is, the more I notice what they have, the less I can see the blessings You have given *me*. I know there are many people with less than what I am complaining about having!

Father God, please help me to see the positive, to enjoy the ordinary and appreciate what I do have, and to not complain about what I don't have in my life. Jealousy and envy cannot change my circumstances, but will only make me bitter. Save me from the "green-eyed monsters" that will steal my joy. If I am focusing on others instead of You, my view becomes blurred. I want to see myself through Your eyes. Please help me to live differently than the world around me.

Teach me to recognize all You have given me and help me to become all You created me to be. Amen.

Let us not become conceited, or provoke one another, or be jealous of one another.
GALATIANS 5:26 NLT

Those Who Wait

Patience. It's certainly not my strength, Lord. When I receive my allowance, I want to rush to my favorite store at the mall to make a purchase. When we plan a family trip, I can hardly wait for the day we leave. And I always begin the countdown to summer vacation at the very beginning of the new school year.

Forgive me for my impatience, Lord. I confess, the same is true when I come to You in prayer. I make a request and wonder if You've even heard me when I don't receive an answer right away. And sometimes I think You've forgotten me or stopped listening to my prayers altogether. But I know that isn't true. Sometimes You say "wait," just like I have to wait for other things in life.

Please help me as I wait. Remind me that faith sees before it receives. You are faithful in Your promises to me through Your Word. I know I can pray in faith and You will answer. It just might not be as fast as I'd like— but I do trust that Your timing will always be perfect.

We do not want you to become lazy, but to imitate those who through faith and patience inherit what has been promised.
HEBREWS 6:12 NIV

Day 18
Living the Faith

"Would I be happy if someone did this to me?" Lord, help me keep that question in the front of my mind every time I do anything to—or for—another person. Let my actions show that I love You. Help me be the kind of girl that not only talks about my faith in You, but lives it!

There are a lot of girls that don't really care about other people's feelings. They've said things about me and my friends that hurt! Help me remember that they probably don't know anything about You and that deep inside they are longing for the love that only You can give. Open doors for me to share Your love with them, even if I don't feel like it at the time. Help me be a good friend and point them to You.

Show me how to live out my faith in You, Lord. Especially when I'm around other kids my age and kids that are younger and look up to me. Help me love—and live—the faith. Amen.

"Do to others whatever you would like them to do to you. This is the essence of all that is taught in the law and the prophets."
MATTHEW 7:12 NLT

Day 19
Is Anyone Listening to Me?

God, do You *really* hear me? There are times when I feel like I'm calling out and no one is listening to me. That most often happens when someone who I thought was my friend betrays me or at times when I feel like I just don't have a friend in this world. More than anything, I want someone to hear me, but my voice just seems to echo back.

But You are a loving God who considers each of His children precious. No one is so far away that You cannot hear them. You not only hear my loud cries, You can hear my softest whisper and even know the feelings inside my heart that I can't form into words to speak.

Help me to remember in those moments when I cry, "No one understands me or even hears me!" that You will *always* hear me and You do care. There is nowhere I can go that You do not see or hear me. I can have the assurance that no matter what happens to me, I will always have a Friend who thinks I'm worth listening to. Amen.

"You are the God who sees me."
GENESIS 16:13 NIV

Day 20
She's Not Like Us

Lord, I hate to admit it, but I sometimes make fun of other people. People who look different. Act different. Have different interests. Hang out with different kids. When I make fun of people who are different from me, I'm so ashamed afterward, but this is so hard! When I'm hanging around my friends, I want to be accepted. So I go along with them when they start poking fun at girls who aren't like us. It's wrong...

I know. Maybe I pay too much attention to what my friends think. Maybe I'm afraid to just be myself.

God, please forgive me for judging others! Help me to remember that "different" doesn't mean someone is worse than me. And please remind me every day that Your Word says we are supposed to be different from the world—set apart, holy. Fitting in isn't the most important thing...being like You is! So when I see people who are different from me, let me see them through Your eyes, Father! You're not looking at the clothes they're wearing or the way they're styling their hair. You are only looking deep inside, to their hearts. Amen.

♥

"The LORD does not look at the things people look at. People look at the outward appearance, but the LORD looks at the heart."
1 SAMUEL 16:7 NIV

Day 21
A Servant's Heart

Dear Lord, as someone who believes in You and what You teach, I am called to a life of serving others and putting them before myself. But because we were all created differently, You have given us different ways of serving each other. Help me to use the gifts and abilities that You have given me in a unique way to serve those around me. I may have gifts that I'm not even aware of! Open my heart to what You would have me do, make my heart sensitive to the needs of others, and give me creative ways to show Your love. Whether it's listening, cleaning, walking the dog, or baking cookies, help me be open to any serving possibilities around me. Thank You for the gifts and abilities that You have given me. Help me not to compare them to anyone else's and to be thankful in everything. Please show me how to serve You, be a good example, and have a servant's heart for my friends, family, and acquaintances. Amen.

The Spirit has given each of
us a special way of serving others.
1 CORINTHIANS 12:7 CEV

Day 22
Lots to Learn

Dear Father, thank You for teachers. Yes, I know sometimes I complain about the homework they assign and the tests they give, but I want to say thank You anyway.

Making fun of teachers is a favorite thing to do with some of my classmates. I feel uncomfortable when they do that, but there have been times I've gone along with it so they wouldn't think I was weird. But I don't think that was right, and I'm sorry. Forgive me for the times I've been disrespectful in my attitude and words about my teachers. Help me keep my mouth shut and walk away when others begin to do that.

Thank You that I live in a country where education is available to everyone. Thank You for the teachers who get up every morning and come to class and answer my questions and grade my papers. Help me show them that I appreciate them. In Christ's name, amen.

Listen to advice and accept discipline, and at the end you will be counted among the wise.
PROVERBS 19:20 NIV

Day 23
Give Me Courage, Please

Heavenly Father, I want to be courageous. Sometimes I face problems that seem too tough to handle. There are times when I'm tempted to do something wrong or when I need to stand for what is right.

I've read about people of courage in the Bible; there was David and Ruth and Daniel and Esther and Mary and Paul and so many more. Lord, these people had confidence in You and knew that You would give them the strength they needed. David was a teenager who fought with a giant and won; Esther was a young woman who went before the king to save her people.

I need that kind of courage and confidence too. Please work in me so I can live for You and bring You glory. I don't want to be weak and cowardly and ashamed of You and Your Word. I want to be bold in my witness for You; I want to live courageously. I ask this in Your name. Amen.

💜

"Be strong and of good courage, do not fear
nor be afraid of them; for the LORD your
God, He is the One who goes with you.
He will not leave you nor forsake you."
DEUTERONOMY 31:6 NKJV

Day 24
God's Delight

You are with me. You are a mighty Savior. You take great delight in me. You will calm me with Your love. You even rejoice over me with singing!

Help me to remember these words in times of fear and stress, heavenly Father. I will need these words to quiet my heart for the rest of my life. You've told me that I'll have trouble in this broken world, but You've also told me to take heart because You have overcome it (John 16:33)! Thank You for this amazing reminder.

I am so happy to know that You delight in me! You look down from heaven, and You smile because You created me and Jesus wiped my sins clean. I don't have to worry that You're angry with me or disappointed. Jesus paid for my sins once and for all (1 Peter 3:18), and I can rejoice in knowing that You see me as a beautiful daughter. Amen.

"For the Lord your God is living among you. He is a mighty savior. He will take delight in you with gladness. With his love, he will calm all your fears. He will rejoice over you with joyful songs."
ZEPHANIAH 3:17 NLT

Day 25
I Believe!

Faith seems like such a simple concept, Father, but it's sometimes the hardest thing to do—believe in something that I can't see. It's not only about the faith that You exist—I take You at Your word, even though I cannot prove it.

But there are many other things that require faith. I trust that when I get into a vehicle, I will arrive safely and on time.

I believe my friend when she promises she will keep the secret that I've kept for so long and finally told her.

I have faith that my parents will supply my basic needs and will take care of me.

I believe everything in Your Word is true and that I should live my life obeying it because that's the only way I will have true success.

Some people will fail me, Lord, and will cause me to lose faith in them; but You have promised that You will never fail me. I can rest in complete confidence that You will always love and protect me. Amen.

Trust in the LORD with all your heart and do not lean on your own understanding. In all your ways acknowledge Him, and He will make your paths straight.
PROVERBS 3:5–6 NASB

Day 26
Who Am I?

God, there are some confusing days in my life. I am trying to figure out who I am and where I fit into this wide world around me. I think about the future and what that will look like—who I want to be when I grow up. I don't want to define who I am by what others say about me. I am who You made me to be.

Ephesians 1:5 says that You adopted me into Your family—that I belong to You! I am not only Your child (John 1:12), but also Your friend (John 15:15), a new creation (2 Corinthians 5:17), and righteous and holy (Ephesians 4:24).

Ephesians 2 describes how my sin kept me separated from You, but through Your Son I am drawn as close to You as possible. Because of Jesus, I am so much more than I could ever dream of being on my own! Help me live with confidence in who I am *in You*. Amen.

But you are the ones chosen by God, chosen for the high calling of priestly work, chosen to be a holy people, God's instruments to do his work and speak out for him, to tell others of the night-and-day difference he made for you—from nothing to something, from rejected to accepted.
1 PETER 2:9 MSG

Day 27
Amazing Love

Father, You love me—and I'm in awe. Even with my many faults and flaws, You care about me.

When I disobey my parents, they get upset; then they usually take away my phone. I sure don't like it when it first happens! But afterward, I realize that my parents discipline me because they love me and want me to learn from my mistakes.

It's so hard for me to wrap my head around the idea that You, Father—a big God, the Creator of the universe—could love and care for me *even when I mess up*! You breathed life into the land, the seas, and me. Your handiwork is all around, and it's amazing…like the first snowfall of the season when I trudge knee-deep through mounds of fluffy stuff or when the flowers and trees bud in the springtime. Sometimes I look into the sky on a summer night, and the moon and star formations are breathtaking! To think that You—the same God who made all of that—love me is beyond my comprehension.

Thank You, Father, for Your constant, unchanging love. Thank You for creating me and giving me new life through Your Son, Jesus. I pray that I will return that love through a life that brings You glory and honor. Amen.

When I gaze to the skies and meditate on Your creation, I can't help but wonder why You care about mortals—sons and daughters of men—specks of dust floating about the cosmos.
PSALM 8:3–4 VOICE

Day 28
Copycat

Lord, I look around at school and at the mall and I see everyone trying to fit in. They copy the styles and actions of everyone they think has it all. I get really confused about this kind of stuff because I want to fit in too. But I want to please You even more. Help me not care so much about what other people think.

Give me a strong desire to please You with a full and thankful heart, knowing that Your plan for me is best no matter what all the other people in my life are doing. I want to be transformed by You into a new person—a girl whose face is radiant and never covered in shame (Psalm 34:5). Amen.

And so, dear brothers and sisters, I plead with you to give your bodies to God because of all he has done for you. Let them be a living and holy sacrifice—the kind he will find acceptable. This is truly the way to worship him. Don't copy the behavior and customs of this world, but let God transform you into a new person by changing the way you think. Then you will learn to know God's will for you, which is good and pleasing and perfect.
ROMANS 12:1-2 NLT

Day 29
I'm Listening to You!

Dear Father, I want the time I spend with You to be moments that I listen to what You have to say, not just give You a list of things I need and want. I know You hear everything I say to You, and it's so easy to pray my "list" of items: help to recall what I need for my test, Your work in a relationship, money to get what I want. . .the list can get really long sometimes.

But, Lord, I want to be better at listening to You. No, it may not be an audible voice, but You can speak in so many ways. You can point out sins that I've forgotten about. You can bring someone to mind whom I need to pray for or even someone I need to share with who doesn't know You yet.

Please, Jesus, help me to be quiet and listen for Your voice. I want to hear what You have to say to me. Amen.

♥

If you call out for insight and raise your voice for understanding, if you seek it like silver and search for it as for hidden treasures, then you will understand the fear of the Lord and find the knowledge of God.
PROVERBS 2:3–5 ESV

Day 30
Collecting Things

Dear Lord, thank You for all the things that You have given me: clothes, a roof over my head, and plenty of fun gadgets. Sometimes I find myself wanting more and more things, and I feel so greedy. You have told us not to store up treasures on earth but to store up treasures in heaven because the things of earth do not last. But it's so hard to remember that when I see a beautiful pair of earrings or a brand-new phone! I don't want to base my self-worth on the things that I have, but it's so easy sometimes to make myself feel better with a new outfit or new technology. Remind me that the things I possess don't have any lasting value and will not bring me closer to You. My purpose in life shouldn't be to collect the biggest and the best things the world has to offer; it should be to glorify You in everything I say and do. Thank You for providing for me emotionally and spiritually as well as physically. Amen.

Then he said to them, "Watch out! Be on your guard against all kinds of greed; life does not consist in an abundance of possessions."
LUKE 12:15 NIV

Day 31
Thankful for My Family

Dear Lord, thank You for my immediate family, for parents who love me and guide me and siblings who play with me and encourage me. And thank You for extended family like grandparents, cousins, aunts, and uncles. You have provided me with such a great support system and so many people who love me and care about me. I realize how much I take them for granted, especially when there are kids out there who aren't as blessed in this area as I am. I pray that You would be their family and their support, that they would turn to You and feel You in their lives. Help me to be aware of people like that in my life and to reach out and love them and be their family. And thank You for friends who feel like family and welcome me into their homes with loving arms. Thank You for being my heavenly Father and watching out for me. Amen.

"Respect your father and mother.
And love others as much as you love yourself."
MATTHEW 19:19 CEV

Day 32
Even When...

I know I'm supposed to honor my parents, Lord. I know it's the right thing to do. But some days, it's so hard! I feel like they don't understand me. At times it feels like they just want to make my life miserable and keep me from things I enjoy.

But Father, I know that's not true. Deep down, I know they love me and only want what is best for me. I also know they're human, and they make mistakes sometimes. And I'm supposed to treat them with great honor and respect, even when they mess up.

Even when I don't understand them, I'm supposed to love and obey them. Even when they speak to me in anger, I'm supposed to speak to them with gentleness and deep respect. Even when it seems like they are strangers to me, who don't have a clue about what's going on in my mind and heart. . .even then, I'm supposed to treat them with honor.

Help me, Lord, to honor You by honoring my parents, even when it's the last thing I want to do. Help me honor them anyway. Amen.

"Honor your father and mother."
EPHESIANS 6:2 NIV

Finding God

I wish I could see You, Lord. I talk to You all the time, but sometimes I don't know if You're really there. I wish there were a place to go, a place to look, where I could find You.

But You said You're everywhere. When I hear birds sing, You're there. When a friend makes me feel good about myself, You're there. When my parents tell me they love me, when I get a good grade on a test, when we have my favorite meal at lunch. . .You are there.

You're not just there in the good things either. You said You'd never, ever leave me. That means when I trip on the sidewalk, You're there. When my friends make fun of me and the tears just won't stop, You're there. When I fail the test I studied and studied for, when I don't get the part I wanted in the school play, when someone I love dies. . .You are there.

I know You are there, Lord, even though I can't see You. When I look for You, I'll find You because You promised to never leave me. Thank You for being there. Amen.

♥

"You will seek me and find me when
you seek me with all your heart."
JEREMIAH 29:13 NIV

Day 34
To-Dos

Too often, Father God, I find the day's chores and homework on the bottom of my *want*-to-do list. I'd rather play games on the computer, talk on the phone with my friends, or watch TV than take out the trash or do math.

But at the end of those days when I do things that only please myself, I find myself feeling guilty because I haven't done what I promised. Then stress sets in because I still have to do all the chores and homework that I neglected to do and bedtime is looming. And neither guilt nor stress feels very good.

I have read in Your Word that "a good woman is hard to find." Yet that's exactly what I want to grow up into—a good woman. One who does her best with everything she puts her hand to. One who doesn't just play around. One who starts her day with an eager desire to please You—not herself—and ends her day feeling good about everything.

Lead my hands to do something more worthwhile, God. Help me make better use of my time. Begin growing me up into a woman who pleases *You*—and in the end herself—in every way, every day. Amen.

A good woman is hard to find,
and worth far more than diamonds.
PROVERBS 31:10 MSG

Day 35
Guarding My Heart

Help me to remember that it is important to guard my heart, Lord. It seems that so many people and things are tugging at it. I fall quickly for the new boy at school. He captures my attention, and I find myself dreaming that he is my boyfriend. I have to fight the temptation to join in with my friends who idolize Youtube stars and musicians. I get easily obsessed with technology and social media. It's like I can't live without constantly texting my friends, but I don't want my heart to be so wrapped up in these things.

When I take a longer look, I realize how worldly some of this is. I want my heart to be focused on my walk with You first and foremost, above anything else that tries to steal my attention. Teach me to be careful with the word "love." I use it too freely: "I *love* this dress!" or "I *love* that kind of pizza!" Create in me a desire to place You above all else in my life. You are my God and my Savior. I love You, Lord. Amen.

Above all else, guard your heart,
for everything you do flows from it.
PROVERBS 4:23 NIV

Day 36
Do What's Right

I'm trying to do what's right, but when I look around, I see others who are getting away with not obeying authority or following the rules. What's with that? When I feel like I'm shortchanged because I'm being the "good girl," should I quit obeying what I know to be right? Even if that's the way it feels, I know that's not what will be pleasing to You, Lord. I also know that's not what's best for me. What's best is doing things Your way.

Lord, help me remember that You honor and reward what is right and that there is punishment for wrongdoing—even if I can't see it. The book of Job says that "the godless seem like a lush plant growing in the sunshine" but "its roots grow down through a pile of stones" and "when it is uprooted, it's as though it never existed!" (Job 8:16–18 NLT).

I want to please and honor You, God. Help me not to look at others, but at You. Help me follow and obey Your Word. Amen.

♥

"But look, God will not reject a person
of integrity, nor will he lend a hand to the
wicked. He will once again fill your mouth
with laughter and your lips with shouts of joy."
JOB 8:20–21 NLT

Day 37
The Royal Rule

One day my friend is friendly, but on another day she seems distant. That kind of rejection makes me feel angry, sad, and confused all at the same time. I know she is a Christian like I am, so it's hard for me to understand how she can treat me like that. Do I ever act the same way and not realize it, Lord?

When a friend treats me badly, I often want to get even. I usually talk to another friend about my feelings, but then that turns into a bad-mouth session, which doesn't end well either. I really want to change how I handle my hurt feelings, Father. Help me to resist creating an excuse to bad-mouth anyone, because when I talk about others I'm disobeying You. Help me to give others grace and to realize that just maybe they've had a bad day and really didn't mean to treat me badly in the first place.

Forgive me for jumping to conclusions just because I think someone has rejected or hurt me. We're all human. Remind me of that, God. Thank You that the Bible gives me clear instructions on what to do when I lose my way—or my tongue! Amen.

Don't bad-mouth each other, friends.
It's God's Word, his Message, his Royal Rule,
that takes a beating in that kind of talk.
JAMES 4:11 MSG

Day 38
Wisdom from
Our Generous God

Heavenly Father, right now I come before You to ask for wisdom. Your Word says that if I ask, and don't doubt, that You will give it to me. Thank You for that promise! Proverbs 28:26 talks about people who trust themselves too much and they are called fools. Forgive me for the times that I think I have all the answers. I don't want to be a fool. I want to be more like You.

Will You search my heart and show me the things in my life that are getting in the way of my relationship with You? I'm confused about some things, and I'd really like to hear from You about them. Please be generous with me and pour out Your wisdom into my heart.

I know I haven't done anything to deserve Your generosity, but I accept that Jesus Christ died for me and that through His power I am considered a precious daughter of Yours. That is amazing! Thank You, Father! Please show me the way I should go (Psalm 32:8).

If you need wisdom, ask our generous
God, and he will give it to you.
JAMES 1:5 NLT

Godly Character

Heavenly Father, I do my best to obey You. I know most of the "rules." I shouldn't cheat, I shouldn't lie, I shouldn't misuse Your name, I should honor my parents....

But my true character would show if I made decisions knowing no one was looking. Would I still keep my eyes off my friend's math exam, or would I sneak a peek if no one could see it? Would I only be honest if someone was watching me, or would I choose honesty even if no one saw? Would I be careful to use Your name when I speak but misuse it in my mind? And my parents...do I only do what they say when they're around, or do I choose to obey and do the right thing even if they're not home?

Lord Jesus, I want to be known as a girl of character. I want to make the right choices simply because it's the right thing to do, no matter who would see it...or if anyone would see it at all. But You see everything, and more than pleasing anyone else, I want to please You the most! Amen.

"The Lord spared me because I did what was right. Because I have not done evil, he has rewarded me."
2 Samuel 22:21 ncv

Day 40
Go for the Gusto

Lord, I don't always feel like working hard. Some days I want to stay in bed late, skip my homework, forget about chores, and just chill. Sometimes I only give half instead of a hundred percent. If my parents ask me to do something, I "sort of" do it but not all the way.

Help me remember that I'm setting an example for others, whether I'm doing the right thing or the wrong thing! The younger kids are watching to see if I work hard, and they're learning from my example. (Oops!) Whenever I'm feeling a little lazy—and I know we all do at times—give me the energy to get up and go for the gusto!

You're a hard worker, Lord! You created the whole earth in one week's time! You still work hard every single day, taking care of people and making sure we're okay. Show me how to be a hard worker like You, Father, one who never ever gives up, even when the going gets tough! Amen.

Being lazy is no different
from being a troublemaker.
PROVERBS 18:9 CEV

Day 41
Loving My Siblings

Lord, my siblings are so annoying most of the time! Sometimes I wish I were an only child so that I wouldn't have to deal with them. When I'm feeling like this toward them, remind me of why I love them and how they have blessed me. Give me patience with them and give them patience with me when I'm being particularly difficult. As we continue to grow up together, I pray that You would bless our relationships with each other and that we would encourage each other to follow You. Not everyone gets a sibling, and even when I'm frustrated with them, I need to be thankful that I have someone to share my childhood with. And help me to look at other people as my brothers and sisters in Christ, that we as Christians are a family who support and encourage each other. Thank You for blessing me with such a great family. Amen.

Respect everyone, and love the family of believers.
Fear God, and respect the king.
1 PETER 2:17 NLT

Day 42
Mirror, Mirror on the Wall

Is it wrong to want to be beautiful, Lord? Sometimes I look at my reflection in the mirror and think I'm pretty. Other times I look away because I feel really ugly. Maybe I spend too much time comparing myself to my friends or to the beautiful ladies in magazines. Help me to see that beauty doesn't really have anything to do with how I look on the outside. When You look at me, You see one of Your daughters, a lovely princess. You don't care if I have freckles or chubby legs.

And speaking of beauty, Father, could you give me a beautiful heart? Sometimes mine gets a little ugly. I let bad attitudes and thoughts mess it up. But I want a beautiful heart so that I can shine like a bright light for You. I'm finally figuring out that being pretty on the inside is more important than the reflection I see in the mirror. May I reflect Your beauty, Father! Amen.

Charm can be deceiving, and beauty fades
away, but a woman who honors the
LORD deserves to be praised.
PROVERBS 31:30 CEV

Day 43
Serving Others

Father, there are a lot of people around me; some deal with physical and mental challenges I can't even imagine. And there are kids who struggle with learning disabilities and social problems and sometimes just strange habits.

Some kids make fun of them, some kids bully them, but others just ignore them. I don't want to do that. I want to show Your love to them.

I remember reading in the Bible about how Jesus healed people when He was on earth. He was kind to everyone; He didn't look down on others because of their challenges. He loved people because they were created in God's image and because they were important in spite of their problems.

God, give me a heart of love for the disabled and severely challenged kids around me. Help me discover ways to notice them and make them feel important. Remind me that my healthy hands and feet and mind are to be used to bless others. Help me reach out in friendliness to those who aren't accepted by the crowd. Give me a servant's heart. In Jesus' name, amen.

Serve one another humbly in love.
GALATIANS 5:13 NIV

Day 44
Gossip

Dear Lord, talking about others is so easy. Sometimes I don't even think about it until after I leave a conversation and consider what I've said. Most of the time I'm not saying very nice things about people when I'm talking behind their backs, and it makes me insecure about what is being said about me when I'm not around. Whenever I'm in a situation where people are gossiping, help me to practice self-control and either keep my mouth closed or come up with something positive to say. I want the words that come out of my mouth to be encouraging and to lift others up, not tear them down and discourage them. Plus, I want my friends to know that I will not speak badly of them when they aren't around. I want to be known for speaking well of others and being a good friend. I don't want to spread lies and hurt others, so help me to think before I speak and love others with the words that come out of my mouth. Amen.

Gossip is no good! It causes hard
feelings and comes between friends.
PROVERBS 16:28 CEV

Day 45
You Made Me

God, lately it seems that every time I glance in a mirror I find something else I'd like to change about myself. I wish I were smaller in some places and bigger in others. I wish I had a different color hair or eyes. I don't like my nose one day, and the next it is my hair that seems all wrong. But then I am reminded that You created me. You put me together in my mother's womb. You decided what color my hair and eyes would be. You formed me to be just the size and shape I am, and You blessed me with gifts and abilities that are unique just to me.

In a way, I guess I am insulting my Creator when I long to look a different way. You made me just the way You saw fit, God, and You don't make mistakes. Deep down, I really am thankful to be me! I would not want to be anyone else. Thank You for making me. Help me to be the very best me I can be. . .for You!

♥

"Bring to me all the people who are mine, whom I made for my glory, whom I formed and made."
ISAIAH 43:7 NCV

Day 46
The Right Road

I have a guilty conscience, Lord. I was asked a question the other day, and I didn't give a completely honest answer. I know there is no excuse for lying—whether it is to protect a friend or even myself.

I also know that part of growing up is to be honest with all people in all things. Yet sometimes, Lord, things, like lies, come out of my mouth before I even know what's happening. But You know what has happened. You see—and hear—all. I know there is nothing I can hide from You and that all will eventually be uncovered. Then I'll have some *real* explaining to do.

So right here and now, I am confessing that I did something wrong. And I am asking for Your forgiveness. I know that talking this out with You is only the first step. Now I need to fess up to those I have hurt with my lies.

Give me the courage to right whatever I've done wrong. Help me to be honest—no matter what the cost. Give me another chance to be faithful to You and Your Word. For I know that when I am walking in Your light of truth, I am on the right road. Amen.

Truth will last forever; lies are soon found out.
PROVERBS 12:19 CEV

A Brand-New Day

Thank You, Lord, for a brand-new day! Yesterday's problems and irritations are over, and today You've given me a fresh start.

Your blessings are new every morning. I can't wait to see what wonderful things the day will bring with You by my side! If something bad happens, help me to rejoice in that as well. I want to praise You *always*—not just when everything goes right, but during difficult times too. I want to praise You in church, at home, at school, and even when I'm hanging out with friends.

Sometimes praising You is a choice I have to make and not a feeling. Father God, I *choose* to give You the praise You deserve. So today, my prayer is that You will keep my heart fixed on You, my thoughts focused on Your promises, and my words overflowing with thanksgiving and gratitude for all that You've done and all that You mean to me.

In the psalms, King David declared that this is the day You have made. He rejoiced in it, and so do I, Lord! Thank You for new beginnings and new opportunities to show my appreciation for all You do. Amen.

This is the day which the LORD hath made;
we will rejoice and be glad in it.
PSALM 118:24 KJV

Too Many Trials

I feel like I have too many trials going on in my life right now, Lord. I don't feel strong enough to handle them anymore. Will You help? I don't feel joyful about them, and I don't even understand how I could! Would You please create in me a clean heart? Would you renew Your Spirit within me (Psalm 51:10)?

I know You would never give me more than I can bear, but the problems I'm going through right now seem dangerously close to being too much. Help me to trust in You more and look at my problems less. Please give me Your peace and strength in the middle of all this stress so that my light will shine for You and my faith will grow.

Will You help me understand what it means to have joy in the midst of trials? I don't really feel very happy with all of this going on, but I can trust that You are in control of all the things in my life. I will trust in You. Amen.

Consider it pure joy, my brothers and sisters,
whenever you face trials of many kinds,
because you know that the testing of
your faith produces perseverance.
JAMES 1:2–3 NIV

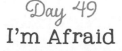

Day 49
I'm Afraid

Lord, I know I shouldn't be afraid because that means I don't trust You as much as I need to. But...I *am* afraid. I don't really know why. It's just that this situation seems so complicated and scary. It's so much bigger than anything else I've experienced. I get my mind all tangled up trying to figure it out.

I'm sorry, Lord. I feel so much better when I put my trust in You and let You take care of my fears and burdens. Please help me not to fear. Help me trust You more. Forgive me for my lack of faith about certain things.

Holy Spirit, remind me of the verse "perfect love drives out fear" (1 John 4:18 NIV) when I'm frozen and afraid. And comfort me with Jesus' words to His disciples when faced with a fierce storm on the sea: "Don't be afraid.... Take courage. I am here!" (Matthew 14:27 NLT).

So Peter went over the side of the boat and walked on the water toward Jesus. But when he saw the strong wind and the waves, he was terrified and began to sink.
MATTHEW 14:29–30 NLT

Day 50
"Frenemies"

Lord, please help me with my friendships! Sometimes my friends act more like enemies. They do things that hurt my feelings. They pretend to be my friend to my face, but when my back is turned, they say bad things about me. I want to be able to trust them, Father, but it's so hard!

Whenever I go through something tough with a friend, please show me how to react in a godly way. You don't like people fighting or talking bad about one another. You want us to be kind and treat people with respect. It breaks Your heart when we pretend to be friends but then treat each other badly.

I know Your Son Jesus went through friendship problems too. One of His best friends betrayed Him. That must've really hurt Him! Still, Jesus forgave him. So help me forgive whenever people go behind my back and do things that bring me pain. I want to learn from Your example, Lord. Help me to be a good friend to others, even when they don't treat me the way I want to be treated. No enemies here, Lord! Amen.

💛

To speak evil of no one, to avoid quarreling,
to be gentle, and to show perfect
courtesy toward all people.
TITUS 3:2 ESV

Day 51
Boring? Ignoring?

It's so hard to listen sometimes, Lord. I just want to tune out my parents when they're talking to me or my teacher when she's standing in front of the classroom teaching us. I'd rather look out the window and daydream! It's hard to listen at church sometimes too. My imagination takes over, and before long I'm thinking about something else, like where we're going for lunch or who's coming over to play. Before long, someone asks me a question and I can't answer it because I wasn't paying attention. Oops!

Would You please help me to not only listen but learn from the people You've put in my life? You put them in my life for a reason, and they have so much to teach me! I don't want to be someone who ignores others; I want to be a girl who cares about what people have to say so that people will care about what I have to say! And help me to listen to Your Word too. I need to pay careful attention because You have so much to teach me. Amen.

"Now then, my children, listen to me;
blessed are those who keep my ways.
Listen to my instruction and be
wise; do not disregard it."
PROVERBS 8:32–33 NIV

Day 52
Loving Myself

Dear Lord, I occasionally find it hard to love myself and appreciate all the gifts and talents that You have given me. I tend to focus on the negative, how I wish I were more like some of my friends and siblings, or I focus on all the things I would change about myself if I were given the chance. I need to remember that I am fearfully and wonderfully made by Your hand—there is no one else that You made like me. Remind me of this fact whenever I wish to change something about myself. I know that I am not perfect and there are things that I could improve on; help me not to get weighed down by my own faults and desires. I trust that You will use me as You see fit, in ways that I might never know about. Thank You for creating me just as I am. I pray that I will continue to grow into a person who shows Your love constantly and encourages others to do the same. Amen.

So God created human beings in his image.
In the image of God he created them.
GENESIS 1:27 NCV

Day 53
Controlling My Temper

Sometimes I have trouble controlling my temper, Lord. Things happen that make me angry, and they happen when I least expect it. At times I don't explode right away, but I hold my anger in. Then it builds and builds through other things that bother me, until finally I explode.

When I'm angry, I say and do things I wish I could take back. I throw fits. I cry. I yell. I try to hurt people. Or I ignore people and refuse to speak to or listen to them. I'm not proud of it, Lord, but that's the way I act when I'm upset.

But when I act that way, it only makes things worse. I need Your help, Lord. I don't always know how to control those kinds of emotions. I don't know how to respond the way You want me to. Teach me; show me how to process my emotions in a positive way that won't hurt others. Give me wisdom and understanding. Help me to respond in love, even when I don't feel like it. And help me to forgive others the way You've forgiven me. Amen.

Because human anger does not produce
the righteousness that God desires.
JAMES 1:20 NIV

Day 54
Good Things

I wonder about my future, Lord. What will I be when I grow up? Will I be pretty? Smart? Happy? I think about these questions all the time.

I know there are things about my future I can't control. I just have to trust You. But there are a lot of things I can control, at least a little. I know if I study hard and make good grades, I have a better chance of getting a good job. I know if I honor my parents now, it will teach me to honor and respect a boss later. If I eat the right kinds of foods and exercise, I'll be healthier, which will make me feel better about myself.

Help me to make wise choices in the things I can manage, for I know those things will contribute to a great future. As for the things that are beyond my control, I trust You. I know You love me. I know You are compassionate and kind, and You have good things in store for me. I love You, Lord. Amen.

Guide me in your truth, and teach me,
my God, my Savior. I trust you all day long.
PSALM 25:5 NCV

Day 55
Your Word Is Light

Thank You, Father, for Your Holy Word which sheds light on my path. This world is full of darkness. It seems that every day I hear more bad news. There is a lot of evil out there. I am so thankful that I know Jesus as my Savior and that I have Your Word to guide me.

I get busy with my friends and activities, Lord, and often I don't spend time reading my Bible. Please remind me of the importance of setting aside time for that every day. Even when I take time just to read a psalm or a chapter or two from the Gospels, I find that I feel closer to You throughout my day. You have given me a guidebook, but it is up to me to read it.

I feel so sorry for those who don't know You, Lord. They don't have the blessing of the light that I have been given. Help me to appreciate Your Word and to seek wisdom from its pages. I love You, Lord, and I want to walk with You all the days of my life. Amen.

Your word is a lamp that gives
light wherever I walk.
PSALM 119:105 CEV

Day 56
What Do I Do Now?

My life is full of decisions to be made. Sometimes I make the right one; sometimes I make the wrong one. I know there are consequences for each of my choices, so why am I drawn toward the things that I know are not the wisest actions?

I want to belong, be part of the group, be recognized and admired. Those desires are not wrong, but if I choose to go against Your way, Lord, then they become a poor decision and can lead to sin—doing things my way instead of Yours.

God, help me to recognize Your way for me, to do what will please You, not others. Happiness is temporary. Joy—which comes from You—lasts forever. Help me make wise decisions in my life. Wisdom from Your Word brings success. It will bring more than I can hope for if I follow it instead of choosing my own path.

Wisdom is using good judgment. It is more than doing what others around me are doing or telling me I should do. It goes beyond just "following the crowd." Help me to make good decisions, Lord—decisions that will please You. Amen.

For wisdom is far more valuable than rubies.
Nothing you desire can compare with it.
PROVERBS 8:11 NLT

All I Really Need

Sometimes I don't have very high self-esteem, Lord. Actually, it doesn't take much for me to feel insecure—like if someone at school is mean to me or a boy I like doesn't like me back or when I fail at something I really wanted to achieve.

I feel like curling up under my covers and staying there *forever*! I don't even want to see or talk to my friends or family. But I'm talking to You, Father, because I know You understand how I feel—no matter how ridiculous my feelings might seem to anyone else.

Please help me to have courage and face my feelings of low self-esteem for what they really are—not based on truth. Help me to see myself through Your loving eyes. Remind me that what others think of me is *not* what defines me. All I really need is Your love and acceptance, and I already have that!

Father, when I start feeling bad about myself and the devil bombards me with negative thoughts, please encourage me with a calm, well-balanced mind. Help me to remember that I am of great worth to You, and that's really all that matters. Amen.

♥

For God did not give us a spirit of timidity
(of cowardice, of craven and cringing and fawning
fear), but [He has given us a spirit] of power
and of love and of calm and well-balanced
mind and discipline and self-control.
2 TIMOTHY 1:7 AMPC

Day 58
Never Ever, Ever Give Up!

Giving up would be the easy thing to do right about now. I'm tempted, Lord. But I'm coming to You for strength. Your Word encourages me in Isaiah 40:28–31 (NLT). Thank You for these verses:

> Have you never heard? Have you never understood? The LORD is the everlasting God, the Creator of all the earth. He never grows weak or weary. No one can measure the depths of his understanding. He gives power to the weak and strength to the powerless. Even youths will become weak and tired, and young men will fall in exhaustion. But those who trust in the LORD will find new strength. They will soar high on wings like eagles. They will run and not grow weary. They will walk and not faint.

What an amazing encouragement Your Word is to me, Jesus! Write this scripture on my heart and help me to never, ever give up!

Then Jesus told his disciples a parable to show them that they should always pray and not give up.
LUKE 18:1 NIV

Make Me Pure

Lord Jesus, there are so many messages telling me that it's okay to try the ways of the world. And it's so easy to give in, believing that others will think I am strange if I don't. But You know what is best. You have told me in Your Word, Father, that You want Your followers to be pure. And something pure can't have just "a little bit" of something bad in it or it isn't pure anymore.

God, please help me to want to be pure. I don't want to do it just to "follow the rules," but because You have asked me to be. You don't tell us to do things because You don't want us to have fun; You give instruction because that's the only way that will benefit us the most and that will result in the best fun!

Thank You, Lord, that even though I may allow impurity into my life at times, I can tell You I'm sorry. You will always forgive me, and You won't hold it against me. Please make my heart and life pure. Amen.

♥

How can a young [woman] keep [her] way pure?
By guarding it according to your word.

PSALM 119:9 ESV

Day 60
Respecting My Parents

Heavenly Father, it's so hard to respect and appreciate my parents sometimes. Even though they have given me everything and love me unconditionally, I still find myself annoyed and wanting to yell at them when I don't get my way or am embarrassed by something they do. When I'm feeling angry or resentful, help me with my attitude and show me how to respect them and love them. They are the only parents I have, and I need to appreciate the ways they sacrifice their wants and desires for me. Thank You for providing me with such wonderful parents. Help me to come up with some ways to show them my respect and appreciation; help me to willingly offer my help when they are working around the house and could use an extra hand. You are the perfect parent, Lord. Even though my earthly parents aren't perfect, I have You, and I am so thankful for Your presence in my life. Amen.

"Each of you must show great respect for your mother and father, and you must always observe my Sabbath days of rest. I am the LORD your God."

LEVITICUS 19:3 NLT

Day 61
Encouraging Others

Dear Lord, I am not always as encouraging as I should be. When my friend is going through a rough time, help me to listen to her, find encouraging things to say, and remind her to turn to You with her problems. When there are annoying situations and others are complaining, give me words of encouragement and optimism so that we aren't dragged down and discouraged. Help me to give generously of my time and abilities to those who need them, and give me encouragement as well. I know it isn't possible to always have positive things to say, but I believe that You have called me to look at things hopefully and to live a life of joy. So with that in mind, sustain me when I'm feeling down and show me how to encourage others genuinely, with honesty and with cheerfulness. Amen.

If we can encourage others, we should encourage them. If we can give, we should be generous. If we are leaders, we should do our best. If we are good to others, we should do it cheerfully.

ROMANS 12:8 CEV

Inner vs. Outer Beauty

How I look means a lot to me! In fact, sometimes I run late for school when my hair doesn't cooperate or I can't find something to wear.

Father, I know that I spend way too much time on how I look. I try different hairstyles and I wear different outfits, yet I'm never satisfied. I experiment with makeup and love to look at jewelry when I shop. Still, I'm not content.

You, on the other hand, focus on inner beauty. Your Word tells me not to worry about the exterior, but to clothe myself with inner beauty. Help me to allow You to change the attitudes or thoughts I have that are ugly and displeasing to You.

Even though I know I'll continue to worry about bad hair days and what I'm going to wear, I want to be who You desire me to be. Father, give me a spiritual makeover! Change me inside. I want Your beauty to shine through me from the inside out because a beautiful spirit radiates even on bad hair days! Amen.

♥

And I want women to be modest in their appearance. They should wear decent and appropriate clothing and not draw attention to themselves by the way they fix their hair or by wearing gold or pearls or expensive clothes. For women who claim to be devoted to God should make themselves attractive by the good things they do.

1 TIMOTHY 2:9–10 NLT

Day 63
Caring for God's Planet Earth

O God, thank You for the world You created. I'm glad for grass and trees and flowers and meadows and forests and mountains; I like rivers and lakes and oceans. You made a pretty place for us to live, and I want to say thank You.

I don't quite understand all the news about climate change and going green and caring for the earth. Sometimes it seems like the people talking care more about the earth than they do about You. I know You want us to respect the world You made and take care of it; it doesn't please You for us to be careless about our waste products and ruin the water and land. But neither does it make You happy for people to save the trees and forget about You.

I want to honor You by being responsible in caring for Your earth, but not worshipping it. Worship belongs to You only. Help me take care of what You created by doing my part. I love the big world You made, and I know that You will keep it right on going until the time You decide. Thank You that I can trust You. Amen.

The sea is His, for He made it;
and His hands formed the dry land.

PSALM 95:5 NKJV

Day 64
A Time of Growing

Growing up is really hard, God; I'm finding that out. My body is changing and so are my feelings about life. I feel awkward and shy around boys now when I used to just think they were dumb. I feel irritable with my mom sometimes, and then I dislike myself afterward. I have trouble saying what I mean when I'm in public; my teeth look too big, and my arms are too long. I think I want to hide somewhere until I've finished all this changing.

I'm learning to take my problems to You, Lord, and this is a big one for me. What does Your Word say about times like this when it seems life is just crazy and you don't know when it will get better? Are there answers for a girl like me?

I know that people in the Bible were once young like me. Even You were once a teenager. Guide me to the places in Your Word that will encourage me and give me hope that this process won't last forever. Help me to believe that You are at work in me. In Christ's name, amen.

He has made everything beautiful in its time.

ECCLESIASTES 3:11 NKJV

Sharing My Faith

God, sometimes when I read Your Word, it seems to be for people more spiritual and wise than I am! I'm just a kid! But then I realize that Your words are for all believers, not just grown-ups. You have given me the Great Commission. It is Your command that I "make disciples." Show me, Father, what this means for a girl like me. I ask You for opportunities to share my faith. Does someone at my school or in my neighborhood need to hear about Jesus from me?

I don't want to wait one more day, Lord, to obey Your command. Give me strength to speak about my faith even when it may not be the popular thing to do. I'm afraid I will say it all wrong, but I know the message is a simple one. Please give me the wisdom and the words I need. I cannot witness to others about Christ in my own strength, but I am willing to try if You will help me. Amen.

"Go therefore and make disciples of all nations, baptizing them in the name of the Father and of the Son and of the Holy Spirit, teaching them to observe all that I have commanded you. And behold, I am with you always, to the end of the age."

MATTHEW 28:19–20 ESV

A Thankful Heart

Lord, my heart isn't always full of thanks. I know You tell us to "be thankful in all circumstances" (1 Thessalonians 5:18 NLT), but that is so hard to do when things in my life are not going right. In fact, some things I'm facing seem unbearable at times. And yet, You still want me to give thanks? That's what Your Word tells me to do, but I can't do that on my own!

How can I be grateful for the difficulties in my life? When my friends don't talk to me or my parents argue or someone I love is sick? And then I remember that through the uncertainties in my life, You remain constant. You are faithful. You will be with me in everything. I can be thankful for that.

I can be thankful for who You are and for all You have done for me—that I am a part of Your family now and that You care for Your own. I can rejoice in knowing that even when I can't understand my situation, You know all about it. Lord, I am thankful that nothing surprises You and that in every situation You can make good things come from bad circumstances. Amen.

Sing praises to the Lord,
you who belong to him; praise his holy name.

PSALM 30:4 NCV

Day 67
Stinkin' Thinkin'

Lord, I realize that what I think about most will shape who I am. But I have trouble thinking positive thoughts. I sometimes think that if I do a certain thing or act a certain way, others won't like me. I focus a lot of energy on my appearance and what I'm going to wear. I take innocent comments personally when I know I shouldn't. I wish I were prettier. I wish I were more popular. I feel like my opinions don't matter to anyone but me.

But, Lord, Your scriptures tell me to fill my mind with beauty and truth. You call attention to inner beauty rather than outer beauty. Please help me to turn my negative thinking around. Shift my thought life to everything that is good, honorable, and true to avoid the traps of stinkin' thinkin'!

When I think about You and how much You love me, I'm so amazed. Thank You, Father, for loving me so much and thinking only good thoughts about me! Amen.

Finally, brothers and sisters, fill your minds with beauty and truth. Meditate on whatever is honorable, whatever is right, whatever is pure, whatever is lovely, whatever is good, whatever is virtuous and praiseworthy.

PHILIPPIANS 4:8 VOICE

Role Model

I really can't believe, Father, that anyone would think of me as a role model. I'm not old enough to be considered one, am I? I mean, my favorite singer is a role model, the pastors in my church are role models, my parents are role models...but *me*? That kind of makes me laugh.

But I guess if I think about it, there are people who could look up to me and want to be like me: younger siblings, kids in the neighborhood, children at church . . .but now it doesn't seem so funny. Now I need to consider whether my words and actions are worth imitating. Have I been a good reflection of You? Am I truly someone a younger person should be like?

Lord Jesus, please help my words and actions be ones that bring honor to Your name. And if I mess up, please help me to make things right so that I can be a good example to those who are younger than I am. Amen.

Let no one despise or think less of you because
of your youth, but be an example (pattern)
for the believers in speech, in conduct,
in love, in faith, and in purity.

1 TIMOTHY 4:12 AMPC

Day 69
Praying for Others

Thank You, Lord Jesus, for the numerous people You have brought into my life. There are so many who have encouraged me and taught me great things. There are also those who have hurt me and been unkind. But, Father, You have made each one of them and love them all the same.

Thank You for the sacrifice and devotion of those who have positively affected my life. I ask that You bless them for their kindness. Please bring them to my mind so that I can not only be thankful for them, but also ask You to work in their lives.

Help me to love those who have caused me pain and sadness. I don't want to avoid praying for them, Father, because of how they have treated me. I want to talk with You about them because I might be the only one who stops to pray for them today.

Thank You for hearing my prayers, Lord. Help me to become more compassionate, praying for those around me—for their physical, emotional, and spiritual needs. In Jesus' name, amen.

I urge you, first of all, to pray for all people.
Ask God to help them; intercede on their
behalf, and give thanks for them.

1 Timothy 2:1 NLT

Day 70
Me? Jealous?

I have a confession to make, Lord. Sometimes I'm jealous of other people. I'm not just jealous of the things they have, I'm also jealous of the way they look or the kind of house they live in. That sort of thing. I'm even jealous of their friendships.

I don't want to be like this, and I know You don't like it either! It's just so hard when I look around and see people who have such great clothes, awesome grades, picture-perfect families, and easy lives. When I'm going through tough times, I look at these other people and I think they've got it made. I know they probably go through stuff too, but it's still hard when I start comparing and wishing we could trade lives.

Jealousy is a sin. I know that, and I'm working on it! Please help me get rid of it. I don't want to be selfish. Not at all. And I don't want to compare myself to others. I know You can change my heart and get rid of these feelings I have. I choose to lay down my "I want what she has" attitude today, Lord. Take my heart and make it clean in Your sight. Amen.

But if you are bitterly jealous and there is selfish ambition in your heart, don't cover up the truth with boasting and lying.

JAMES 3:14 NLT

Day 71
Strong and Courageous

I don't always feel strong, Father. Some days I just want to hide in my closet, away from anything that scares me. School. Relationships. Problems in my family. Friendship struggles. Scary stuff. Sometimes I pretend I'm courageous, but in my heart I'm so terrified! I don't want people to know what a scaredy-cat I am, but it's true!

Can You make me strong, Lord? I know the Bible says You can! You say that I can be strong and courageous, like David facing the giant, Goliath! But even David didn't have the courage to slay Goliath on his own. He needed Your strength, Father.

That's what I'm asking for today—Your strength. I put on Your armor and take up my sword and shield (my Bible) and march forward like a brave warrior, headed into the enemy's camp. I know You will go before me, and that gives me all the courage I need. With Your help, I will be victorious! Amen.

"Be strong and very courageous. Be careful to obey all the law my servant Moses gave you; do not turn from it to the right or to the left, that you may be successful wherever you go."

JOSHUA 1:7 NIV

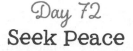

Day 72
Seek Peace

Girls can be mean, Lord. We're supposed to be all pink and fluffy and sweet, but we have a vicious side too. I don't know why, but it seems like whenever a group of my friends gets together, someone gets their feelings hurt. Then we all end up taking sides, and before you know it, there's an all-out war. That's what it feels like, anyway. Things are said, tears are shed, and I just hate it.

I'd like to say I'm innocent of that behavior, but I'm not, Lord. I'm just as guilty as my friends of saying something mean and hurtful, of taking sides, of making the battle bigger than what it needs to be. I'm not proud of it, and I don't want to be that way.

I want to be a peacemaker. I want to help everyone get along, not contribute to the fighting. But I don't always know what to do or how to act or what to say to make things better. I need Your help, Lord. Give me Your wisdom today and every day to know how to bring peace to difficult situations. Amen.

Seek peace and pursue it.

PSALM 34:14 NIV

Day 73
Thoughts about Romance

Father, I'm starting to think about romance; it will be cool to fall in love someday with a good-looking guy. I'm glad You thought up the idea of guys and girls and falling in love and marriage. You were the One who created Adam and Eve and put them together. You decided to use marriage as a symbol of Your love for Your people. The people who believe in You are called the Bride of Christ, and You say that Your return for us will be as exciting as a wedding day. So I know that romance is a pretty special idea.

Lord, I want to have my own romance someday. In the fairy tales, the princesses are loved by a strong, handsome prince. I want to fall in love with a wonderful man and have a beautiful wedding day and live happily ever after. I ask You to help me know the man that You want me to marry; help me guard my heart and not just give it away to anyone. And thank You that even if I never marry, I can be loved by You, and that love will last forever. Amen.

"Yes, I have loved you with an everlasting love."

JEREMIAH 31:3 NKJV

Healing Power

I want to offer a prayer today, Jesus, for sick friends and family members. I know that You healed so many people when You were here. So I ask You now, Lord, to apply that same healing power to the ones I love.

Go to them now, Jesus. Allow them to feel Your presence. Touch them with Your amazing hands. Calm their fears. Give them the courage to face their challenge, to have hope in Your love. Pour out Your wisdom on their doctors.

I don't really understand why some people have to suffer, Lord. But I know that You have a wonderful plan for each one of us. And so I trust in You and surrender my worries. I am putting their lives into Your big, strong, mighty hands.

Increase the faith of my loved ones who are hurting. And if they don't know You, I pray that their eyes would be opened. That they would see You for who You truly are—a great and loving God.

Thank You, Lord, for all that You have done for us here on earth and for all that is waiting for us in heaven. Amen.

He heals the brokenhearted
and bandages their wounds.

PSALM 147:3 NLT

God's Love

God, it seems that things are always changing in my life. Just when I think things are going to stay the same, something else happens that's out of my control. I find myself fearful of change. I don't want to lose anything or anyone in my life. There is just no guarantee that things will remain secure and stable. It can really be confusing sometimes, and even scary.

Thank You for assuring me through Your Word that nothing can change Your love for me. No matter where I go, You are there. No matter what changes take place in my life, one thing will remain steadfast, and that is the deep love You have for me. When I am afraid, remind me of Your love. Comfort me and teach me to run to You when my heart is troubled or when I feel like life is spinning out of control. Thank You, Lord, for loving me with a love that will truly never let me go. Amen.

I am sure that nothing can separate us from God's love—not life or death, not angels or spirits, not the present or the future, and not powers above or powers below. Nothing in all creation can separate us from God's love for us in Christ Jesus our Lord!

ROMANS 8:38–39 CEV

Day 76
God Will Never Leave Me

People fail me. My friends don't always understand me, my family can't be there for me every single moment, and teachers and other adults may not follow through on their promises. No one is perfect except You, God. You will always be there for me.

I know that even though my family and friends may *want* to be there for me, it is not always possible. So rather than focusing on them, help me depend on You. In moments when I feel alone, help me recall Your words of truth and comfort from the Bible: "Even if my father and mother abandon me, the LORD will hold me close" (Psalm 27:10 NLT). When others abandon or fail me in some way, I need to turn to You, Lord.

On days when I feel forgotten or overlooked, remind me that I can count on You, Lord. You won't leave me. You won't abandon me. Help me to know I am not alone. I can always reach out to You in prayer. Thank You for being the one I can turn to, for being there for me even when others are not available. Amen.

God has said, "I will never leave you;
I will never abandon you."

HEBREWS 13:5 NCV

Guide Me, Lord

I'm so confused, Lord. My thoughts run this way and that, and I don't know what to think sometimes. There are days when I need some solid advice and guidance. Okay, I admit I need guidance *most* of the time!

Father, You promised to guide me on the best path for my life. You said You'd watch over me and give me good advice. I'm asking for that right now, Lord. I need Your guidance as many temptations and problems bombard my thoughts and circumstances run out of my control. How should I act? What should I do? Which direction should I take?

Thank You, Father God, that Your direction is perfect and Your judgments are wise. I praise You for the guidance You give me daily as I seek You in prayer. It amazes me that You often give me wisdom beyond my years!

Lord, I want to follow You and continue to seek Your will and ways throughout my lifetime. Please guide me on the pathway You've set just for me. Amen.

The Lord says, "I will guide you along the best pathway for your life. I will advise you and watch over you."

Psalm 32:8 nlt

Day 78
God Hears Me

God? Can You really hear me? Sometimes I feel like my prayers are only hitting the ceiling and not making their way to You. I want to have a deep relationship with You, knowing that You are a constant presence in my life.

Please search my heart and show me anything that I'm doing or thinking right now that is getting in the way of our communication. Please hear my prayer and set me free from any burdens that I'm carrying that I really don't need to be worried about.

Speak to me through Your Word. Let Your words be the answers to my questions and a light to my path (Psalm 119:105). It amazes me that when I read and memorize Your Word, You bring it to my mind later at just the right time when I need to hear from You. This helps me trust that You really do hear me and care about all the little and big things in my life.

Thank You for hearing me and loving me, heavenly Father. Amen.

Out of my distress I called on the LORD; the LORD answered me and set me free.

PSALM 118:5 ESV

Day 79
Changing My World

Father, I want to do great things for You! There are so many people with big needs all around me. Some are in desperate need of financial help. Others could really use my help in doing physical work that they are unable to do themselves. Some would benefit from volunteering my time in service. And others just need a friend who can sit and spend some time with them.

Sometimes I may prefer to use my time on my own needs and desires. It may take my time, my money, or my physical labor to make a difference in someone's life. But I am grateful for the times that others help me, and I want to be available to help others. More than anything, I want to meet the needs of others so that Your light shines through me.

Please, Lord Jesus, help me to be aware of people in my world who I could assist. And then give me the strength to help them out—not to receive recognition, but rather to be a light for You. Amen.

Do not neglect to do good and to share what you have, for such sacrifices are pleasing to God.

Hebrews 13:16 esv

Day 80
Wonderfully Made

Father, the Bible says that my body is the temple of God. I guess that means I should stop and think about the things I'm putting in it. I have to confess, sometimes I eat junk food. Too much junk food! There's so much tasty stuff to pick from, after all! Sometimes I don't pay attention to whether or not it's good for me. If it's yummy, I eat it! And I also have to confess that sometimes I don't really feel like exercising or taking care of myself. I'm too tired or too busy. It's easier to lie around on the sofa and watch TV or play video games.

You made me, Lord, and I know You want me to take care of myself. The Bible says that I'm "fearfully and wonderfully" made, which means I'm really important to You. I guess that also means that I should take care of my body so that it will stay healthy and strong. I want to live a long life and grow up healthy and strong, so help me make a plan to watch what I eat and to exercise so that I can do that! Amen.

I praise you because I am fearfully and wonderfully made; your works are wonderful, I know that full well.

PSALM 139:14 NIV

Day 81
Big and Little Stresses

Dear God, I stress out about so many things, big things like what I am going to do with my life and little things like homework and social stuff. It's easy to come to You with the big stuff because You are a big God and I know that You care. But it's hard for me to bring the little things like a test I'm worried about or a boy I like, because those seem so small in comparison. But I know there is not one problem or complaint that I have that is too small for You, because You care about everything in my life. Remind me that I can talk to You at any time and any place about what is bothering me. You care for the birds of the air and the beasts of the field. Because You take such care with those small creatures, it gives me confidence in Your care of me. Thank You for those examples of Your love and care. Amen.

God, examine me and know my heart;
test me and know my anxious thoughts.

PSALM 139:23 NCV

When I'm Afraid

Sometimes I feel afraid, Lord. I know I'm old enough that I shouldn't feel afraid, but I do. I'm scared of all sorts of things.

I'm afraid of being laughed at or rejected by my friends. I'm afraid of not doing well at school. I'm afraid I'll mess up and make my parents feel ashamed of me. I'm afraid of bullies. But You said as long as I trust in You, I don't have to feel afraid. You'll be with me in everything I do, and You'll help me and protect me.

I know I still have to make wise choices. I can't do foolish things, like go off with strangers or run into a busy street, and expect You to protect me. But I also know that if I'm following Your leadership, You'll never leave me. You'll keep me safe from harm. . .and even when harm comes my way, You'll help me through it. I don't have to fear as long as I'm trusting You and holding on to Your promises.

Lord, please replace my fear with a calm assurance that You have everything under control. Amen.

When I am afraid, I put my trust in you.

PSALM 56:3 NIV

Day 83
Keeping Things Orderly

I don't like chores, God—making my bed, loading the dishwasher, running the vacuum, doing the laundry. I confess I don't always have a good attitude when my mom asks me to help her, and I'm sorry about that.

I know, God, that You like things orderly too. The Bible says that You created all things and You did it in a certain order. And then You put certain things in place to help things stay orderly—like the laws of gravity and space and the ocean tides and sunrises and sunsets and seasons. I like having order in my life; it would be terrible if we just floated everywhere like in outer space or if one year we skipped summer. I'm glad I can depend on things to stay in place like You made them.

So, I need Your help not to be grumpy about my chores. When my mom needs me to help her, I want to be cheerful and not complain. Remind me that I am pleasing You when I obey and when I keep things in their place. And I'm sure glad I can trust You to keep all the big stuff running correctly! Amen.

♥

He existed before anything else,
and he holds all creation together.

COLOSSIANS 1:17 NLT

Day 84
A Unique Purpose

Lord, sometimes when I dream about the future, I see myself doing so many different things—from designing fashions, to nursing, to writing bestselling books. My ideas change from day to day. There are so many things a girl can do and be!

Yet I know You have created me for a unique purpose. You have set me here at this exact time, space, and place for a reason. And although I am not sure yet what that is, I know that one day You will show me exactly what You've had in mind for me all along.

Help me not to worry about the future but to continue to explore this world and my someday role in it. I know You have a plan for me. Help me not to worry about which road to take. Remind me that You know exactly where I'm heading and will give me signs along the way—in Your own good time. Meanwhile, I will do my part to be patient, trusting, and watchful. Amen.

"For I know the plans I have for you," declares the LORD, "plans to prosper you and not to harm you, plans to give you hope and a future."

JEREMIAH 29:11 NIV

Day 85
Family

God, You gave me the family I have. Regardless of whether we look like other families, this is the one You provided for me. I want to be thankful for them and not compare myself to others. We might not look the same or act the same as other families, and sometimes they may drive me crazy, but they are my family.

When I start comparing myself to others and see areas I would like to be different, I also have to see what I have that others don't. No family is perfect. (I'm not perfect!) Help me to appreciate the good things and to change the things I can about myself to help make my family better.

Lord, the things I can't change are the things I have to trust to You. Right or wrong, there is so much not in my control. I can only make decisions for myself, not for anyone else. When I become discontent with who I am and where I came from, I want to look for all the positive areas of my life. Help me recognize the people You have placed around me to love me and help me. Amen.

Exploit or abuse your family, and end up with
a fistful of air; common sense tells
you it's a stupid way to live.

PROVERBS 11:29 MSG

Day 86
Looking Good

Clothes are important—I don't want to look like a weirdo! But what I think is cool or fashionable, I'm not always allowed to buy or wear—even if everyone else is wearing that style. That's so old-fashioned; sometimes it doesn't seem like the adults in my life get it.

I care about what others think of me, God, but maybe I should care more about what *You* think of me. Isn't it more important what is on the inside than the outside? How I dress matters to me, but what I haven't thought about until recently, God, is that it matters to others and can impact their lives too. I want to look cool, but I understand that modesty is important also. Luke 12:27 tells us that You "clothed" the lilies in the field, and look how beautiful they are!

Maybe what I am wearing matters most of all to You, God. Help me find clothes that I like but also that are pleasing to You. Amen.

"Don't fuss about what's on the table at mealtimes or if the clothes in your closet are in fashion. There is far more to your inner life than the food you put in your stomach, more to your outer appearance than the clothes you hang on your body."

LUKE 12:22–24 MSG

Day 87
God Gives Me Strength

What does it mean to be strong, Father? I cry when someone hurts my feelings or when things in my life go wrong. I don't mean to pout or act like a baby, but sometimes I let my emotions get the best of me.

You and Your disciples showed a lot of strength. You preached the Gospel even when the authorities disliked it. You stood up for what was right and true. I too want to be Christlike. I want to be strong in my faith and convictions.

Lord, only You can give me the strength to stand fearless in uncomfortable situations. Help me to grow stronger each day—physically, spiritually, and emotionally—so that I can be the person You created me to be. Give me victory over life's fears and frustrations.

Meanwhile, I know I can rest in You, confident that You are working in my life. To know that I can walk in Your strength is a comfort to me. You've put a song in my heart and victory in my steps. So I can smile. . .no matter what. Amen.

The LORD is my strength and my song;
he has given me victory.
PSALM 118:14 NLT

Beautiful Inside and Out

There are so many people I would consider beautiful, Lord Jesus, but in all honesty, there are days that I don't feel like *anyone* could use the word "beautiful" to describe me. I don't feel as if I can measure up to the level of beauty all around me. The images on TV, in the movies, and in magazines are so perfect, and I can't come close to that.

Forgive me, Father, for judging my worth by what my hair or face looks like, how much I weigh, or the kind of clothes I wear. You are the master artist and have designed me just the way I am. Please don't let me get so caught up in the world's standard of beauty. I do want to take care of myself and look the best I can, but I also need to work on being attractive on the inside too. Please help me to focus on being what I need to be in Your eyes, not to the eyes of those around me. Amen.

♥

"Looks aren't everything.... GOD judges persons differently than humans do. Men and women look at the face; GOD looks into the heart."

1 SAMUEL 16:7 MSG

Day 89
I Love You, Lord!

Father, it's so easy to say I love something or someone. I constantly find myself saying I love a certain kind of food, a TV show, my favorite actor or musician, an article of clothing I see at the mall, or even my friend's nail polish. I guess I can overuse the word "love" at times.

But God, I do love You. You have made me unique, and You have promised to meet my needs. I can trust You with my deepest secrets and know that You not only hear me but care about me too. You only want what's best for me.

Thank You, Jesus, for loving me first and for loving me so much that You came to earth to die for me. That is the ultimate love! I love You so much too. I'm sorry for the times I don't show that love and seem to take our relationship for granted. My heart is full of love for You, and I want to grow in my love for You more every day. In Your name, amen.

"Love the Lord your God with all your heart and with all your soul and with all your mind and with all your strength."

MARK 12:30 NIV

Caring for Those in Need

My heart gets so heavy when I see people who don't have a place to live or food to eat. Whenever we drive by a homeless person, I feel sick inside. Should I give him food? Water? A blanket? I never know what to do, Lord. Can You show me? Are there people in my church or my community who need my help?

Lord, give me eyes to see the needs of people all around me—the elderly neighbor who needs a friend. The little boy with cancer. The lady across the street who has no time to spend with her kids because she's always working. How can You use me to help out? Can I offer to clean? To fix a meal? To start a fund-raiser? Whatever You ask me to do, Father, I will do! I want to reach out to those in need as You've told me in Your Word to do. Amen.

Suppose a brother or a sister is without clothes and daily food. If one of you says to them, "Go in peace; keep warm and well fed," but does nothing about their physical needs, what good is it? In the same way, faith by itself, if it is not accompanied by action, is dead.

JAMES 2:15–17 NIV

Day 91
Stress Express

Between all the schoolwork, sports, fun with friends, stuff with family, and other activities, Lord, I feel super stressed out. There are only so many things I can do in one day. When I am pulled in so many different directions, I get really cranky. And it's all because I feel as if I am riding on the stress express!

Lord, show me how to arrange my activities, beginning with what's most important—spending time with You. When I feel frazzled and totally out of energy, lead me to Your side. I know You have a place where I can be at rest, where all is still. In Your presence, I can get things straight in my head. I find new direction and strength. I am refueled.

Allow me to take time right now to rest in You. As I close my eyes, I see myself lying in a wonderfully green meadow. The sun overhead warms me. Beside me is a pond where the water is very still. Here, I am at peace. Here I am—with You. Amen.

He makes me lie down in [fresh, tender] green pastures; He leads me beside the still and restful waters. He refreshes and restores my life (my self).

PSALM 23:2–3 AMPC

Day 92
Not Funny

Why does everyone think it's funny to put people down, Lord? It seems like the more my friends know how to insult people, the more popular they are. People say mean things, everybody laughs, and suddenly everyone wants to be the mean person's friend.

But I don't think it's funny to insult people. It's hurtful to the person being insulted. Even if they laugh on the outside, I know they're hurting inside. I know because it's happened to me. I've pretended to be fine with the hurtful comment, but the unkind words have stayed with me long after the laughter died down. I've even cried into my pillow at night over some of those not-so-funny comments.

Help me not to fall into that trap of saying mean things just to get a laugh, Lord. I don't want to cause others to hurt the way I've hurt. I want to be a person people feel safe with, a person people know will be kind no matter what. Teach me to be an encourager. I want to build people up and make them feel good about themselves. Amen.

Therefore encourage one another and build one another up, just as you are doing.

1 Thessalonians 5:11 esv

Day 93
I Hate Divorce

Dear God, I'm mad about divorce. I wish moms and dads would stay together forever.

Divorce makes everything confusing; there are two homes instead of one and two sets of rules and two kinds of food, and it's hard to go from one to the other. Divorce means you can't spend your holidays with both parents, and that just stinks! Divorce means you cry yourself to sleep at night and feel empty and sad inside.

God, I know that divorce happens and that it's not the kids' fault. But it is terrible to have a family that is all broken up and has to try to be nice to each other in public. I know You made families to stay together, but Satan doesn't want it that way. He is happy when families split up.

I'm so glad that You can be there to help hurting families; thank You for being there to hear prayers and bring comfort. Be with everyone who is sad today because of divorce; let Your love be felt. Help me to be careful when I choose a husband someday and to be committed not to divorce the man I marry. I ask this in Jesus' name. Amen.

♥

He heals the brokenhearted
and bandages their wounds.

PSALM 147:3 NLT

It's Not Fair!

Life isn't fair. I see so many things every day that just aren't right. It seems like evil wins and nobody cares. But I know *You* care, God. Jesus showed His love over and over again for those who were helpless—those who had no control or power to make their lives different. He loved the lame and the sick, the widows and orphans. He told His disciples to let the children run to Him.

I know Jesus' arms are open wide to everyone. He loves even the unlovable and died for *every* person—even those who hate Him. What's fair about that? God, You are holy. We are not. It is only by Your Son's sacrifice that we can know You. By Your standards we deserve to be separated from You, yet because of Your great love for us through Jesus, there is a way we can be with You forever even though we don't deserve it! What's "fair" about that? Lord, thank You that life is not fair—but You are! Thank You for making a way for me to know You through Your Son. Amen.

"Still, you keep on saying, 'The Master's way isn't fair.' We'll see, Israel. I'll decide on each of you exactly according to how you live."

EZEKIEL 33:20 MSG

Popularity

I want to be popular, God. I want to be one of the girls everyone admires. I know it may not be the right way to feel, but it's the truth. I long to be part of the "in" crowd, and some days I would do almost anything just to make sure I'm noticed.

I guess it's more important to look for those who love You and whose hearts are on the same path that mine seeks to follow. I don't want to wake up one day and be popular but not have Christian friends around me who can encourage me to do what is right. Sometimes I get afraid of being swept away into things that I know do not honor You. . .all because I desire so desperately to be popular.

Clean up this way of thinking in me, God. Show me the right kind of friends, those who love You. And then if others do notice me, help me point them to You. Help me, God, not to be so worried about being popular. Amen.

The righteous choose their friends carefully,
but the way of the wicked leads them astray.

PROVERBS 12:26 NIV

Doing My Best

Sometimes I just can't get too excited about doing the boring tasks I have to do every day. I mean, who cares, right? It's just the same old routine. Yet You tell us in Colossians 3:23 that we should do the best work we can—to work as if we are doing it for You, not for people.

Doing ordinary things well doesn't seem like it amounts to much, but in Matthew 25 You promise that those who are faithful in the small things will be rewarded. Does that include simple things like cleaning my room and doing my homework?

God, I want to succeed—I want to *be* the best at something. But what if my best isn't good enough—or if I'm not really good at anything? Philippians 4:13 (NKJV) says, "I can do all things through Christ," so then I guess it's not about what I can do, but what You can do through me. So help me do my best for You, Lord. Not for others or even myself. Help me to see that the small things are important simply because You say they are. Amen.

Observe people who are good at their work—skilled workers are always in demand and admired; they don't take a backseat to anyone.

PROVERBS 22:29 MSG

Day 97
True Success

Expectations. What do people expect of me? What do I expect of myself? More importantly, what do You expect of me, Lord?

I know that everyone has expectations. I have hopes and dreams for my future, and sometimes I wonder if those dreams will ever come true. My parents expect me to achieve good grades and follow Your teachings, Father. I want those things too.

I want to know You more, Father God. I want to be successful not only in my physical life, but in my spiritual life as well. I want You first in my life because that's true success. You said to seek the kingdom of God and Your righteousness, and everything else will fall into place!

Please nudge me to read the Bible and spend time with You every day, Lord, before I do anything else. So many things draw me away from quiet time with You. I desire to seek You with all of my heart. And I know that if I do, You will take care of all the other needs in my life. Amen.

"But seek ye first the kingdom of God, and his righteousness; and all these things shall be added unto you."

MATTHEW 6:33 KJV

Day 98
From Sorrow to Joy

I'm really down, Father. I seem to have no hope. I have lost someone close to me, Lord. And I don't know when things will be the same again.

Some days I feel so sad. I don't know what to do. How long will it take for this wound to heal—a week, a month, a year? I need something to hang on to, something to help me get through these next days.

Open Your Word to me. Lead me to a new hope. Give me the courage to keep going. Lift the weight of sorrow from my heart. Help me to take things one moment, one hour, one day at a time, knowing that You are holding my hand through it all. Show me how to praise You, for I know that when I do, I will suddenly feel better.

In the meantime, give me the strength and the willingness to help others, for when I do, I am lifted out of my sorrow.

Thank You for what You are going to do in my life and for the joy that will someday be following this sorrow. Amen.

I would have lost heart, unless I had believed
that I would see the goodness of the
LORD in the land of the living.

PSALM 27:13 NKJV

Day 99
Never Give Up!

Dear Jesus, it seems as if I hear the expression "Never give up!" all the time. It's a short saying that I think about when I'm exercising, studying for my finals, or trying to reach another of my many goals. But even though it sounds like a simple thing to do, it's actually really difficult—especially those times when it would be so much easier to just give up. Sometimes I think I just can't make it.

Thank You, heavenly Father, for giving me the strength I need at those times when I'm weak. I know what waits for me at the "finish line," but the work getting there wears me out. If I try it on my own, the results aren't usually what I was hoping for. But You have promised to carry me through when it's tough, so I ask for Your help in reaching my goals.

I don't want to give up, Lord. Help me keep my eyes on You and on the benefit I will receive from finishing well. In Jesus' name, amen.

Do not let yourselves get tired of doing good.
If we do not give up, we will get what is
coming to us at the right time.

GALATIANS 6:9 NLV

Leaving a Legacy

Wow, God! Sometimes I think about my parents and grandparents and great-grandparents, and I see this long line of people that I'm part of. How cool is that? And how amazing to know that one day I will probably have children and grandchildren and great-grandchildren too. They will be part of a great big family that started a long, long time ago.

It's so awesome to think that You knew me even before I was born, just like You knew my parents and grandparents before they were born. I guess that must mean You know more about me than anyone, even my own family. That also means I can trust You because You're the One who designed me in the first place.

Thank You for taking the time to create me, Lord. I want to leave a legacy, to be remembered as part of something bigger than myself. Help me to do that by the way I live and the way I worship. Amen.

The word of the LORD came to me, saying, "Before I formed you in the womb I knew you, before you were born I set you apart; I appointed you as a prophet to the nations."

JEREMIAH 1:4–9 NIV

Day 101
Voices

I hear so many voices throughout the day. I listen to my parents, my teachers, my brothers or sisters, my friends, my coach, my pastor. . .everyone! Sometimes I become frustrated with so many people telling me what to do and when to do it.

Yet I know most of these voices are channels of truth and love in my life. I love the voices of the very people who sometimes irritate me because I know they love me and want what's best for me. Trusted adults give me lots of advice that I need as I grow.

But sometimes I need time alone, apart from all the voices and chaos. I enjoy spending time alone in my room where I can focus on my own thoughts. I think about things in my life, and I think about You, Father. When I'm alone is when I hear You the most, during those moments when I can just talk to You without interference from anyone. It's then that I can open my heart and tell You how I feel.

Yours is the only voice I never tire of. It is gentle, soothing, and refreshing to me. I want to hear Your voice more. I need to! Lord, as I pray, please help me to listen. When I read the Bible, show me the words I need for my life. Amen.

Be still, and know that I am God.
PSALM 46:10 NKJV

A New Song

Some days I find myself complaining about everything, Lord. I don't mean to, but sometimes everything just seems to get on my nerves. I don't know if I got out on the wrong side of the bed or if life is really out to get me. But whatever the reason, those days just aren't any fun.

But I don't have to complain, do I? I can choose to look for the positive in any situation. Help me to see the good in things, Lord, even when life doesn't go my way. I want to be one of those people who keeps a smile on her face even when circumstances are tough. I don't want to be known as a whiner or a complainer.

You said You'd put a song in my heart if I look to You. That's what I want, Lord. I want to be so content, so filled with Your love that I'm always singing, even if it's just inside my head. Next time I feel like complaining, help me to sing a song of praise instead. Amen.

He put a new song in my mouth,
a hymn of praise to our God.

PSALM 40:3 NIV

Honor Your Father and Mother

God, Your Word tells me that I should honor my father and mother, but what about when they make mistakes or do something wrong? What if I disagree with them? How do I honor someone when we are so far from being on the same page, we're in different books altogether? Is honoring different than obeying? And do I have to agree with everything they tell me? When I have a different opinion, does that mean I no longer honor them?

Honor means respect, and respect means "paying attention to" or having "a high or special regard for." When I listen and acknowledge what my parents say, I have respect for them. I can honor their position as my parents, and I know I have to obey them. Even when my opinion is different than theirs, I need to speak politely and not be angry. That's hard sometimes, Lord.

Help me understand what it is to honor and obey my parents without losing my own ability to think for myself and to always be respectful. Amen.

Children, do what your parents tell you. This is only right. "Honor your father and mother" is the first commandment that has a promise attached to it, namely, "so you will live well and have a long life."

EPHESIANS 6:1–3 MSG

Day 104
Right Here, Right Now

Lord, I find myself confused, unhappy, and lost—all because I have been neglecting You and Your Word. You have been waiting outside my door, knocking, and I have not let You in. And now nothing is going right.

Suddenly I realize that it's not You but me who has moved!

So here I am, Lord, right here, right now. At this moment, I am imagining You sitting right next to me. Forgive me for being so caught up in other things. Give me the peace, strength, direction, and hope I need to live the life You have planned out for me. Help me to be more loving to myself, my family, and my friends. In this moment. . .

I give You my heart to have and to hold. Cleanse it of worry.

I give You my mind. Fill it with good thoughts.

I give You my life. Lead me where You would have me go.

I give You my all as I rest in Your presence. Speak to me. I'm listening. Amen.

"See! I stand at the door and knock. If anyone hears My voice and opens the door, I will come in to him and we will eat together."

REVELATION 3:20 NLV

Day 105
A Masterpiece

I sure don't feel like a masterpiece, God. I sometimes feel more like a mess! Your words in Ephesians 2:10 have been such a comfort on a day like today! Just to know that in spite of all my failures and flaws, You think I'm great! How can it be? You are a holy God, and I'm so imperfect. I feel like I ruin everything, and I certainly feel unattractive most of the time.

But You gaze at me and smile. I am Your daughter, Your precious child, Your masterpiece. Give me the ability to do the good works that You have created me to do. Show me Your will and Your way for my life, and give me courage to follow You even when I'm not sure where You are taking me. I am Yours, God. And wow, it feels amazing to be valued by the God of the universe! Thank You for making me, for loving me, and for stamping me with Your approval—just because I'm me, just because I belong to You. Amen.

For we are God's masterpiece. He has created us anew in Christ Jesus, so we can do the good things he planned for us long ago.

EPHESIANS 2:10 NLT

Don't Judge Me

I hate it when people decide things about me that aren't true. They make a "judgment" about my clothes, where I live, the color of my hair or skin, the way I talk or look. They assume I am something based on their own false ideas of what any of those things say about me. It hurts to be misjudged or treated as "less than," especially when I know other people don't really know me.

But if I'm honest, Lord, I guess I would have to say I might do the same thing. If I'm not careful, I can make judgments about others based on what I believe to be true, but it's possible to not have the full story or to have an opinion without all the facts. I really don't want to do that!

Help me to see people for who they really are—not what they look like or even what they do. God, help me to treat others as I want to be treated. Amen.

💙

"Don't judge others, and you will not be judged. Don't accuse others of being guilty, and you will not be accused of being guilty. Forgive, and you will be forgiven."

LUKE 6:37 NCV

Day 107
The Truth!

Father, forgive me when I lie. Sometimes when I'm put on the spot, it seems easier to lie than to tell the truth. Immediately, I know I've sinned, and I regret it. I realize that if I continue to lie, I will become more likely to repeat those lies; eventually, lying will become a sinful habit. And lies only lead to trouble!

Lord, Your Word tells me that the devil is the father of all lies. But I belong to You. You are my heavenly Father, and I am Your child because Your Spirit lives inside me. Please help me when I'm tempted to lie—no matter how hard it might be to tell the truth. Even in those moments when I'm afraid of the consequences, remind me to do what's right.

I ask that my words reflect You, Father. Give me uplifting, honest, caring words as I speak the truth. I surrender my will to You. I surrender my thoughts and words to You too! Amen.

So put away your lies and speak the truth to one another because we are all part of one another.

EPHESIANS 4:25 VOICE

Day 108
A Walk Down the Runway

Okay, I'll admit it, Lord…I pay a little too much attention to what people are wearing sometimes. I like pretty clothes and jewelry. Looking through magazines for fashion ideas can be fun. It feels good to dress up and look pretty. People notice when I wear a cool new outfit, and that's very flattering.

I don't want to get too carried away with it, though. Fashion can be a fun distraction, but it doesn't need to be my main focus. I ask You to remind me daily that it's not what I wear on the outside that matters, but the condition of my heart. Remind me too of all the girls around the globe who don't have money to buy new clothes or shoes. To You, they are just as beautiful, even if they don't have fancy things to wear. Amen.

For women who claim to be devoted to God
should make themselves attractive
by the good things they do.

1 Timothy 2:10 nlt

Day 109
My Life Is Yours

Dear Father, I have to admit that when I hear the word *surrender*, I think of someone who loses because they gave up. It doesn't sound like something a person who is strong and in control would do.

But Your definition of *surrender* isn't like that at all. Yes, it does mean giving up, but not in a weak sort of way. You want me to give up my "me first" thoughts and give You first place in my life.

I'm sorry for the times I have tried to take things into my own hands and do things on my own. That never seems to work out for the best. I know the safest place for me to be is in Your care because You see the "big picture" of my life and know what's best for me.

Lord Jesus, I want to surrender my whole life to You. I want You to have complete control. Help me to recognize the times I try to take over so that I can ask for Your forgiveness and follow Your way. In Your name, amen.

Therefore, I urge you, brothers and sisters, in view of God's mercy, to offer your bodies as a living sacrifice, holy and pleasing to God—this is your true and proper worship.

ROMANS 12:1 NIV

Me and My Big Mouth!

Oh, my big mouth! Lord, sometimes it gets me in trouble. I don't mean to spout off, but sometimes I feel like a teakettle, overflowing with hot water and covering the whole room! I get upset, and things just come racing out of my lips before I can even think them through. Before long, I've "burned" all sorts of people with my ugly words.

Forgive me for this, Lord, and help me change. Make my words gentle, Lord. May I follow Your example of loving others, showing courtesy to all the people I know.

I know that You want me to guard my tongue, Father. Help me with this! I need to know how to react when I'm faced with a situation that's tough. I don't want to spout off like that teakettle. I want to react calmly. And when I do speak, I want my words to be kind and loving, not angry and mean. Amen.

To speak evil of no one, to avoid quarreling,
to be gentle, and to show perfect
courtesy toward all people.

TITUS 3:2 ESV

Day 111
My Selfishness

Dear Lord, I can be so very selfish in every area of my life. I am selfish with my time, my possessions, my friends, and a lot of other things. I don't want to constantly think only of myself; I want to be unselfish and serve those around me in any way that I can. Make my heart sensitive to the needs of those around me, and make me alert to my own selfishness, especially when it comes to helping others. You have said that the greatest commandments are to love You and to love my neighbor as myself; help me to do both of those things in my daily life. It is so much easier to be selfish and to just curl up with a book instead of helping my mom in the kitchen or raking the yard with my dad. And it's even hard to share things with my siblings, but I know those are things that You would have me do. Thank You for never being selfish and being the perfect example of serving others. Amen.

Do nothing out of selfish ambition or vain conceit. Rather, in humility value others above yourselves, not looking to your own interests but each of you to the interests of the others.

PHILIPPIANS 2:3–4 NIV

Delight in Him

There are so many things I want, Lord. New clothes, new gadgets, new stuff for my room. . . And whenever I actually get something I want, there's always another item to take its place on my wish list.

I want things for my life too, Lord. I want to be popular. I want to make good grades. I want to be the best at the things I love to do. Sometimes I want those things so much it hurts.

But You said I'm supposed to want You more than I want anything else. I'm supposed to delight in You. I guess that means You're supposed to be the One that makes me happier than any of my stuff, happier than any of my goals.

I do delight in You, Lord. I know You love me, and that makes me smile. But I know I could think about You more. I know I could spend more time doing things I know would make You happy. Help me, today and every day, to delight in You. I know being close to You is the best thing I could ever wish for. Amen.

Take delight in the LORD, and he will
give you the desires of your heart.

PSALM 37:4 NIV

Grandparents Are Great

Dear God, thank You for thinking of the grandparent idea. It was a really great thing. I'm so thankful to have grandparents who love me and teach me and are there for me through anything.

My grandparents still show off my picture to strangers and sometimes embarrass me with their hugs, but they're really cool anyway, and I know they want the best for me. When I've had a hard day at school, they understand and let me talk it out. When I visit them, they buy special food for me and let me stay up late.

I wonder if Jesus knew His grandparents. I know it was different for Him because He was really Your Son, but maybe He had a special relationship with his earthly grandparents too. It's really cool that You understand the things about my life that way.

So I'm saying a prayer of thanks for my grandparents and also praying for them. Please take care of them and keep them healthy and let me have them in my life for a long time. Help me to be a good granddaughter. I ask this in Jesus' name, amen.

Grandchildren are the crowning glory of the aged.

PROVERBS 17:6 NLT

Love God and Love Others

God, You've made Your purpose for me pretty simple, and I'm so thankful for that! Love You...and love others. Help me to focus on that each and every day and not get caught up on rules and laws. I trust that if I'm growing in my love for You and for the people in my life, You will teach me all that I need to know through Your Word and through the people around me that love You too.

I won't lie, because You know the truth in my heart: there are some people I know that are really, *really* hard to love! Will You help me do a better job at that? I fail a lot in that area, especially when I get frustrated with certain friends and family members.

Thank You, Jesus. I love You. I'll do my best to love others too—with Your help! Amen.

If anyone boasts, "I love God," and goes right on hating his brother or sister, thinking nothing of it, he is a liar. If he won't love the person he can see, how can he love the God he can't see? The command we have from Christ is blunt: Loving God includes loving people. You've got to love both.

1 John 4:20–21 msg

Day 115
God Will Take Care of Me

Lord, the future frightens me. The next year of school …the unknowns about what I will be doing… What if it's too hard or too much for me to handle? What if I don't have any friends? The what-ifs are overwhelming. I try to turn off my brain and not get anxious, but I am really scared at times. I wish I had a crystal ball that could show me the days to come and assure me that I will be okay.

How silly of me to think like that! Remind me that You are much better than a crystal ball with no powers at all. You are the powerful God of the universe, and You have promised to take care of me! You keep the earth spinning on its axis. You clothe the fields with grass, and You even feed the birds. How much more You value me as Your child, created in Your image! I know that You will be there every step of the way and that if I look to You, You will provide all that I need. Thank You, Lord, for this promise. Amen.

"Look at the birds. They don't plant or harvest or store food in barns, for your heavenly Father feeds them. And aren't you far more valuable to him than they are?"

MATTHEW 6:26 NLT

Day 116
I Am Wonderful!

You made me wonderful! Thank You that I can say that not in an arrogant way but in a way that gives me confidence to live out a life that pleases You, Lord!

You created me.... You decided what I would look like.... You blessed me with certain gifts and talents that only I possess.... You gave me a purpose...and You set Your Spirit inside me when I asked Jesus into my heart! What more could a girl ask for?

I don't need to worry about what other people think about me, because I know what You think about me, Father God! Everyone else seems to look at outside appearances only, but I feel blessed and deeply loved that You look at the inside of my heart and call me Your daughter.

Thanks for making me beautiful in Your eyes—and help me to smile like I believe it! Amen.

"Bring the ones who are called by My name; the ones I made, shaped, and created for My profound glory."

ISAIAH 43:7 VOICE

The "In" Crowd

Lord, I want to fit in. It feels good to belong to a group. Some groups are a bad influence on me, so I need Your help with that, God.

When You walked the earth, the disciples were Your closest friends. You did everything with them, and they learned so much from You. In fact, You chose the disciples for Your companions while still interacting with and serving unbelievers.

Protect me from the wrong friends while prompting me to serve others as You say I should. Give me the strength to stand apart from the girls who are bad influences and who could hinder my relationship with You.

I admit that sometimes I go along with the crowd just so I will be liked and accepted. I want to fit in, and instead of standing up for what's right, I remain silent.

Help me to seek out other kids who have a strong Christian faith, Lord. Bring friends into my life who can help strengthen my spiritual growth and not diminish it. Most of all, when I'm around kids who don't know You, help me to love them and pray for them. Help me to be a good influence in their lives so they can see how You've made a difference in mine. Amen.

Do not be deceived:
"Evil company corrupts good habits."

1 Corinthians 15:33 nkjv

Even So, I Praise You!

Father God, what is Your divine plan for my life? What do You want me to do? What shall I become? What does my future hold, Lord? I wonder about these questions when I think about my life and my relationship with You.

I wish I had all the answers and didn't have to wait for them. But that's not how You work, Lord. Help me to take one day at a time, one step at a time, instead of trying to rush through the years.

The Bible does tell me I can know one thing for sure about Your will for my life: namely, that I should give thanks in *every* circumstance. Wow...not a particularly easy thing to do, because not everything I go through is an awesome experience. In fact, some things in life are just plain awful. Yet You made it clear that I am to show my appreciation to You—no matter what I'm going through—to praise You *in* my circumstance, not *for* it.

I know You don't invite bad things into my life, Father; but I can thank You despite them. Is that what You meant by giving thanks *in* all circumstances? Even so Lord, I praise and thank You, no matter what my day brings. Amen.

Give thanks in all circumstances; for this is
the will of God in Christ Jesus for you.

1 THESSALONIANS 5:18 ESV

Study Help

I sometimes wonder if all the studying is worth it, Jesus. I feel like my life is a constant cycle of waking up early, getting ready, going to school, coming back home, and doing loads of homework. I feel like I hardly have any time for fun!

But, Father, I know You want me to do my best in everything I do, which includes my schoolwork. Help me to have a better attitude about it and want to do a good job—not just barely pass. The time I put into it will determine my grades, so I know that for now I need to work hard to get through my classes—even that one I could really do without!

I ask for Your help in getting through these classes. Help me, please, to study what I need to and for the length of time that I should. Please teach me how to avoid distractions so that I can reach my goals and finish well. . .so I can even have some fun time when the work is done. Amen.

Do your best to present yourself to God as one approved, a worker who has no need to be ashamed, rightly handling the word of truth.

2 TIMOTHY 2:15 ESV

Day 120
Tough Stuff!

Life is so hard sometimes, Lord! I know You already know this. Your Son, Jesus, went through a lot of hard times. He was betrayed, rejected, made fun of, and then put to death on a cross. I can't even imagine what that must've been like. I know You understand what it's like, and You care.

The problem is, sometimes I think I don't have enough energy to get everything done. Schoolwork. After-school activities. Family stuff. Church obligations. I feel like I'm in over my head sometimes. How can I possibly get everything done and still get a good night's sleep?

Show me what's important to do, Father. I don't want to do stuff just to stay busy. I want the "stuff" I do to be important to You. So, if there's anything in my life I'm not supposed to be doing (please say homework, Lord!), show me. Help me to create a schedule that works for me and my family, one that leaves me plenty of time left over to pray and spend time in Your Word. Amen.

From the ends of the earth, I cry to you for help
when my heart is overwhelmed. Lead me
to the towering rock of safety.

PSALM 61:2 NLT

Day 121
Pride

Dear Lord, help me to be humble. I find it so easy to be prideful sometimes, and I know that is not honoring to You. When I take pride in my grades or my success in sports or my appearance, I need to remember that You are the one who has given me these abilities and that I should be humble and thankful for what You have given. I know there is nothing wrong with being confident in the gifts that You have given me, but I don't want to brag and base my self-worth in things that I do. I want to be humble and serve others and glorify You. You have said that the last shall be first and the first shall be last; help me to remember that when I put myself before others. When I'm tempted to brag or take too much pride in something, please humble my spirit and remind me that everything I have is a blessing that comes from You. Amen.

Too much pride can put you to shame.
It's wiser to be humble.

PROVERBS 11:2 CEV

Not Alone

Sometimes I feel so alone, Lord. I know I have people around me who love me, but they don't always understand me. They don't know my thoughts or why I do the things I do. I don't even understand myself a lot of the time, Lord. And it's a lonely place, feeling like nobody gets you.

But You made me, Lord. You know my thoughts, and You understand things about me that I don't even understand about myself. And since You promised You'd never leave me, that You'll always be with me, I know I don't have to feel alone. I'm always in the company of the One who knows me better than anyone and who loves me just the same. I know Your eyes are always on me, and You always hear me when I talk to You.

Help me remember that, Lord. I want to feel Your presence with me. Walk with me as I go through my day. Whisper Your words into my mind. Remind me that You are always there so I won't have to feel alone. Amen.

The eyes of the LORD are on the righteous,
and his ears are attentive to their cry.

PSALM 34:15 NIV

Day 123
No More Death

O God, I wish people didn't have to die. Some people I love have died, and I miss them a lot. It's hard to keep going when you're very sad. Every day looks cloudy even if the sun is shining, and you don't want to laugh or hang out with friends; you just want to cry.

I know that death is the result of sin coming into our world long ago when the first couple, Adam and Eve, disobeyed You. I know You didn't mean for us ever to die. I wish there weren't funeral homes and caskets and cemeteries. But there are, and I need You to help me deal with it.

Thank You for the hope of heaven for those who believe in You; thank You for sending Your Son to pay for my sins so that I can live forever with You where there is no death.

Be with me when someone I love dies; help me remember to bring my pain and fear to You. Give me hope and remind me to trust You. And someday take me to live with You forever. In Jesus' name, amen.

"And God will wipe away every tear from their eyes; there shall be no more death, nor sorrow, nor crying."

REVELATION 21:4 NKJV

Day 124
Peace and Harmony

I come to You today, Lord, with a troubled heart. How am I to handle bullies, people who pick on me or others? And bullying comes in so many forms—from hurtful words to painful actions. What's a girl to do?

I know You don't like it when people stir up trouble or when innocent people are picked on. So I ask You to give me the wisdom to be kind to everyone and the courage to walk away from people who say or do mean things.

Put Your wall of protection around me. Shield me from the hurtful words of others. Give me Your eyes so that I can see the good in all people. And fill me with the strength to lend a helping hand and to lift up those who are weak.

I pray for peace—at home, at school, and in our neighborhood. Show us all how to live together in harmony. Amen.

♥

There are six things the LORD hates, seven that are detestable to him: haughty eyes, a lying tongue, hands that shed innocent blood, a heart that devises wicked schemes, feet that are quick to rush into evil, a false witness who pours out lies and a person who stirs up conflict in the community.

PROVERBS 6:16–19 NIV

Day 125
"I'm Sorry"

Lord, there are times when I lose my temper and end up saying things I don't really mean. Then there are other times when I mock someone just to make my friends laugh.

What I'm trying to say is that there are situations—more than I'd like to fess up to—when I say or do the wrong thing and an apology on my part is definitely needed. So, Lord, bring to my mind all those I have wounded. For all these mistakes I've made, all these people I have hurt, whether or not on purpose, please give me the courage to go to them and say from my heart, "I'm sorry." I know that is the right thing to do. And although the words *I'm sorry* may not fix everything right away, they are a beginning.

Once I have done my part to heal a rift, then, and only then, will I feel ready, willing, and able to come and worship You with a clean heart and a clear conscience. Amen.

"If you enter your place of worship and, about to make an offering, you suddenly remember a grudge a friend has against you, abandon your offering, leave immediately, go to this friend and make things right. Then and only then, come back and work things out with God."

MATTHEW 5:23–24 MSG

Day 126
That Makes Me So Mad!

Oops, I blew it, Lord! I said some things that I know I shouldn't have—and truly wish I hadn't—but the words just slipped out. As much as I want to, I can't take it back. The damage is done. Now I have to repair the relationship. It's really hard sometimes to think about the other person's point of view. The thing is, even if I am right about the situation, the results are not what I wanted!

Proverbs 18:21 (MSG) says, "Words kill, words give life; they're either poison or fruit—you choose." I do choose, Lord—even when my emotions can seem out of control, I still have a choice what comes out of my mouth. Help me to say what I want to say without destroying others in the process. I know I hate harsh words when they are directed at me, so help me to speak kindly even when there are difficult things to express.

Thank You that I can come to You with what I am feeling, God. I know You understand and can help me handle my anger. Amen.

A gentle answer deflects anger,
but harsh words make tempers flare.

PROVERBS 15:1 NLT

Role Models

Lord, forgive me for placing celebrities on a pedestal. I know they are only people—just like me—but their celebrity status seems to elevate them in my mind somehow. I purchase magazines that feature popular musicians and bands so I can learn more about their personal lives; I also plaster posters of my favorite celebrities on my bedroom walls.

Father, Your servant Paul told the early Christians to follow his example as he followed the example of Christ. I know I should choose Christian role models who live their lives for You. Even though the world bombards me with temptations and influences of the rich and famous, I ask that You change my heart to desire only Your ways and Your will.

Surround my life with more of You, Jesus. I want to follow You; I want to be like You. Forgive me for often allowing the world's influences to speak to my heart. Give me godly role models; and help me become a good role model too. Amen.

Follow my example,
as I follow the example of Christ.

1 CORINTHIANS 11:1 NIV

Day 128
No More Comparing

My friend has beautiful hair and a perfect complexion, God. But I look in the mirror and see pimples and frizz. Sometimes I wish my teeth were straighter and that my face wouldn't break out at the sight of chocolate. I'm sorry when I get down about this stuff, Lord. Would You give me Your perspective?

I believe that when You look at me You see something beautiful that You created. You smile at me and are pleased by my appearance. Would You please help me to see myself the way that You see me? When I compare myself to my friends, I get very insecure. I start to feel bad about myself and freak out trying to make myself look like everyone else. Please forgive me for that, and set my heart and mind back on You.

You look into my eyes and call me beautiful. You know the number of hairs on my head (Luke 12:7), and You even count my tears (Psalm 56:8). Thanks, God. My heart belongs to You alone. Amen.

But when they measure themselves by one another and compare themselves with one another, they are without understanding.

2 CORINTHIANS 10:12 ESV

Discipline

It's just not fair, Lord! I shouldn't be grounded! I didn't do anything wrong!

Well, I guess the more I think about it, it *was* the wrong thing to do. I did what I was told not to do, and they found out. But the grounding was way too harsh!

I have to take a deep breath, Father, and first ask for Your forgiveness. Then I need to go and make it right between them and me. That's going to be so difficult! Especially with *this* punishment!

But even though I think it's unfair, I need You to help me be respectful—not to try to get an easier punishment, but because You want me to honor those in authority over me. You've put them in that position, so I need to respect that. . .and even be thankful for it. Thank You for giving me people who care enough about me that they want me to make good choices. And please help me to make better choices in the future! In Your name, amen.

♥

There is no joy while we are being punished.
It is hard to take, but later we can see that
good came from it. And it gives us the
peace of being right with God.

HEBREWS 12:11 NLV

Day 130
Light and Life

There are so many dark things in our world today, Lord. I know You see it. It has to hurt You seeing what so many people that You created are doing to themselves and to others. Knowing what some kids my age are doing right now is scary. And watching the news is even scarier!

Will You use me to be a light in a very dark place? Please transform my life to be all that You want me to be. Help me to follow Your will for my life without grumbling and complaining. There are certain things I know I have to do as part of growing up: go to school, do chores, be responsible, help my family. Sometimes I don't like all the responsibilities I have, but help me to carry them out with love and light in my heart.

Help me to hold fast to Your words, Lord. When so many around me are living in the dark, let me be light to them. Amen.

❤️

Do all things without grumbling or disputing, that you may be blameless and innocent, children of God without blemish in the midst of a crooked and twisted generation, among whom you shine as lights in the world, holding fast to the word of life.

PHILIPPIANS 2:14–16 ESV

Day 131
Anxiety

God, I find myself being anxious about everything in my life. I worry about my grades, my friendships, my clothes, what I will do in the future, whether or not I'll ever have a boyfriend, the list just goes on and on. Whenever I'm worrying about things that are beyond my control, help me to remember Your words: "Do not be anxious about anything." I need to tell myself that in every situation. You are present, and You are looking out for me. You have provided for every living thing on the earth, so why should I doubt that You will take care of me? You said in Matthew 6 that only people who don't know God worry about such things. Help me to entrust my anxiety to You, to not take on the cares of tomorrow, and to lift everything up to You in prayer. You will never leave me or forsake me, and that assurance should remind me not to worry. Amen.

Do not be anxious about anything, but in every situation, by prayer and petition, with thanksgiving, present your requests to God.

PHILIPPIANS 4:6 NIV

Trouble Everywhere

Lord, sometimes it seems like everything that could go wrong does go wrong. I spill orange juice on my favorite outfit right when it's time to leave. My best friend decides she's mad at me. My parents make me clean my room again when I thought it was clean, and my little brother won't stop bugging me. On top of it all, I forgot there was a science test and didn't study for it. I feel certain I failed.

Some of these things I don't even have control over, Lord. Like my little brother bugging me and my best friend being mad and not telling me why. I feel like troubles are falling on me from every side, and there's nothing I can do about it.

But I know You're with me, Lord. No matter what happens, at least I don't have to face it alone. At least I know that as I deal with hard things, You're right beside me, holding my hand and giving me wisdom to get through them.

Thank You, Lord, for loving me enough to stay with me even when things are hard. Thank You for giving me the wisdom to get through even the most difficult situations. Amen.

The righteous person may have many troubles,
but the LORD delivers him from them all.

PSALM 34:19 NIV

Can't Take It Back

Lord, my mouth got me in trouble today. I said some terrible things to my friend, and she was so hurt. After I said it, I wanted to take it back, but I couldn't. I feel awful, and I need Your forgiveness, please.

I'm learning, God, that my words can be helpful or hurtful. It's very easy to make another person feel bad by saying something unkind. There are bullies who like to make other kids afraid by the things they say. I don't want to be like that. And then there are some others who always say something mean just because they think it makes them look cool. I don't want to be like that either.

I want to be in control of what I say even when I'm upset. I know that the fruit of the Spirit is self-control, and I sure do need it. Help me not to be used of Satan to hurt others, but instead let me encourage them and make them feel loved and happy.

Thank You for forgiving me; I'm trusting You to help me remember this so I will be more careful next time. In Christ's name, amen.

Too much talk leads to sin.
Be sensible and keep your mouth shut.
PROVERBS 10:19 NLT

Day 134
Prayer

Heavenly Father, You are the best listener in my life!
Yet so often I forget to take advantage of Your listening
ear. I run to my mom or my best friend and completely
forget to pour my troubles out to You. Thank You for
providing me with people in my life whom I can talk to
about things, but help me to remember that You want
to hear about things too. And I forget that prayer can
be a conversation. I need to listen for You; You may not
say anything, but You do make Yourself heard in my
life. I can talk to You anywhere, anytime. When I'm by
myself, remind me of that fact. I can talk to You when
I'm walking the dog or taking a bike ride. I can even talk
to You silently when I'm surrounded by people, like on
the bus after school or during youth group. Thank You
for Your constantly listening ear and for all the ways
that You encourage me and are patient with me. Amen.

Each morning you listen to my prayer, as I bring
my requests to you and wait for your reply.

PSALM 5:3 CEV

My Thoughts

I want to be a "glass half full" type of girl, Lord. Sometimes I view it as "half empty," don't I? I often become self-absorbed and make too much of my worries and troubles. It seems that I am down and disappointed far too regularly.

I need Your help to control my thoughts. Help me to take every thought captive to Jesus as Your Word encourages me to do. When Satan tries to convince me that I am not worthy of love or that I am not good enough, please stand between my mind and his wicked schemes. Father, chase those thoughts away. Protect my mind and train me to dwell on the positive, the lovely, the blessings in my life. Help me to trust in Your truths rather than fall for the evil one's lies. I want to think on excellent, noble things. I want to walk in right paths and not become entangled on wrong ones that will lead me to destruction. Be the Lord of my thought life, I ask You today. Amen.

Finally, brothers and sisters, whatever is true,
whatever is noble, whatever is right, whatever is
pure, whatever is lovely, whatever is admirable—
if anything is excellent or praiseworthy—
think about such things.

PHILIPPIANS 4:8 NIV

Standing Up for Others

I hear it every day—people talking about other people. And usually what they have to say isn't very nice and probably isn't even true! While I try not to gossip about others, sometimes I find myself in that awkward place of being around people who do—and wondering exactly how to handle that.

I don't want to come off as if I think I'm better than they are, God. I just don't want to be part of tearing someone down. Especially when I know that one of my friends (or even I) could be their next target. So what do I do, Lord? Give me the words to speak in those situations.

I want to honor You and also honor others. I want to think the best of people. And I definitely don't want to spread rumors! Even if something is true, that doesn't mean it needs to be shared. Help me encourage the people I'm around to not talk negatively and to speak truth not lies. Amen.

Who may worship in your sanctuary, LORD?
Who may enter your presence on your holy hill?
Those who lead blameless lives and do what is
right, speaking the truth from sincere hearts.
Those who refuse to gossip or harm their
neighbors or speak evil of their friends.

PSALM 15:1–3 NLT

Day 137
Love or Bear a Grudge?

Father God, when someone does something to hurt me, like gossip behind my back or make a nasty comment, I get angry and hold a grudge. In my heart, I seek revenge even though I know it's the wrong way to feel.

I know that in life some people are mean-spirited. Yet how I react to them is what counts. Lord, I can't love someone like that without Your power and strength. In fact, I don't even *want* to love them. I want them to feel as bad as they have made me feel.

Please change my heart so that I can see them as You do. You loved even the greatest of sinners. In fact, You died for them and for me. If You could endure death on the cross for the people who persecuted and mocked You, how much more should I forgive those who have hurt me?

Help me to learn from Your example and not seek revenge or harbor bad feelings; rather, empower me to pray for those who have hurt me—and yes, to love them with Your love. Amen.

"Do not seek revenge or bear a grudge against anyone among your people, but love your neighbor as yourself."

Leviticus 19:18 niv

Loving My Enemies

I don't know if I have many enemies, Lord. But I do know there are a lot of people that don't like the fact that I'm a Christian. They don't believe in You, and they are looking for any chance they can to dispute Your existence and make me feel stupid for believing.

Help me to love them anyway. And help me to do good to them in any way that I can so that they might second-guess their thoughts about You. Let them see little glimpses of Your power and love through me.

Your Word tells me that my fight isn't really against flesh and blood; it's actually against the devil and his evil schemes (Ephesians 6:10–13). Help me to be strong in You and in Your mighty power. Use me to bring light and love into the darkness. Amen.

♥

"Love your enemies! Do good to them. Lend to them without expecting to be repaid. Then your reward from heaven will be very great, and you will truly be acting as children of the Most High, for he is kind to those who are unthankful and wicked."

Luke 6:35 NLT

Day 139
Joy vs. Happiness

Lord Jesus, thank You for the great things that happen in my life—the ones that make me so happy. After something absolutely wonderful happens, I close my eyes and try to relive the moment, to keep feeling that wonderful feeling.

But then some days seem so. . .plain. Nothing great happens. And other days are just plain awful. Why can't I be happy every day?

Father, help me to remember the difference between happiness and joy. At times I think the words mean the same thing, but they really don't. Happiness is a result of what happens to and around me. But joy—*true* joy—comes from knowing that You love me so much and care about what happens to me. So even on the absolute worst of days, I can still have joy in my heart because I have You in and with me.

I want to live a life full of joy, Jesus, and want others to see that I'm different. Because even when bad things happen, I can still have a spirit of joy and rest in Your goodness. Amen.

And so my heart is glad. My soul is full of joy.
My body also will rest without fear.
PSALM 16:9 NLV

Day 140
The Best Book of All

Reading a good book is so much fun, Lord. I love adventure stories, where the hero saves the day. I also like stories set in the olden days, before I was born, because they help me know what life was like back then. I especially like to read books about people who've been through struggles, because I learn from what they've been through. It helps me know I'm not the only one who goes through stuff. Yes, a great book can totally lift my spirits!

Thank You, Father, for the best book of all—one loaded with more adventure, more history, and more personal stories than any other. Your Word—the Bible—is action packed! Wow! I learn so much when I take the time to read it. Remind me every day how important it is to read this amazing book and to pray for those who haven't had a chance to read it yet. I can't wait to see what happens next, Lord! Amen.

"This book of the Law must not leave your mouth. Think about it day and night, so you may be careful to do all that is written in it. Then all will go well with you. You will receive many good things."

JOSHUA 1:8 NLV

Day 141
Telling the Truth

Lord, help me tell the truth no matter what. I don't like to think of myself as a liar, but sometimes it's easy to stretch the truth a little or tell just a teensy lie to make myself look better or to keep from getting in trouble.

But when I tell one lie, I often have to tell another to cover the first one. Then another and another. Before I know it, I'm buried in a pit of lies, and I don't know how to get out.

Even when the lie stops at just one, I feel bad. I'd rather be the kind of person who has integrity. The kind of person who tells the complete truth, even if the truth might hurt me. In the long run, I'd rather be known as a trustworthy person. The only way to earn trust is to consistently do the right thing. And that includes telling the truth.

I know You value honesty. I know that when we lie and we get caught, it causes others not to trust us. I don't want to get in the habit of saying things that aren't true, even if they don't seem that important. Help me to speak the truth today and every day. Amen.

An honest answer is like a kiss on the lips.

PROVERBS 24:26 NIV

Day 142
Knowledge Is Cool

Sometimes I don't like school, heavenly Father! I get tired of writing papers, taking tests, and studying.

My mom says I need to be thankful that I can learn. I know there are girls in other countries who can't attend school. I guess it would be really sad to want to learn and not be able to. So I am thankful that I can read and write my name and have a chance to learn the stuff I'll need for life; I just feel a little grumpy about school in general today.

I wonder if Jesus went to school when He was a boy on earth. The Bible doesn't tell us, but He probably did. Wow, wouldn't that be scary for the teacher if he had known that he was teaching the Son of God?

Well, Father, I'm going to choose to stop complaining and just get my homework done. It's not a lot of fun, but I know it's good for me to learn. Thank You for giving me a mind that can understand and for all the help You give me as I open my books and study. You're an awesome tutor! Amen.

The fear of the LORD is the beginning of knowledge, but fools despise wisdom and instruction.

PROVERBS 1:7 NIV

Day 143
My Best for You

Heavenly Father, slackers get on my nerves. You know who I'm talking about, right? . . . They do the bare minimum—scraping by just enough to get a passing grade, whether it's geography, art, history, or math. Extra effort? They're certainly not giving it!

Sometimes I need to remember that whole slacker thing for myself. I mean, I know You gave me special gifts and abilities, but that doesn't mean I should do less than my best just because certain things are beyond my comfort zone, right? If science isn't my thing, I still should make an effort to learn it. And just because I'm not a long-distance runner doesn't mean I should walk the entire mile in gym class.

God, please help me to remember that every opportunity I have comes from You. And You expect me to give my all in *everything* I do. Please bring to mind every area in which I'm tempted to slack off—and keep me accountable, Lord, so I tamp down all temptation to give less than 100 percent. Thanks, God! I know You won't let me down! Amen.

Don't you realize that in a race everyone runs,
but only one person gets the prize? So run to win!

1 Corinthians 9:24 nlt

Behind the Scenes

Lord, sometimes my heart is full of doubt. With so much trouble in the world, I wonder where You are and why You don't do something!

Yet I know You see and hear all. Nothing escapes You. And when I look into Your Word, I see the amazing stories of all that You have done for us on earth. Deep within, I know that Your Word is truth. It is there I find Your power to heal, move mountains, shake the world, strengthen the weak, and feed the hungry. There is nothing You cannot do! And there is nothing *I* cannot do if I have faith. Often You are working behind the scenes. I am sure You have saved me from many hidden dangers. Every day I feel blessed for what You have given me—friends, family, food, fun.

Right now I feel Your presence within me and all around me. And it is here, in You, that I have victory! Amen.

"If you embrace this kingdom life and don't doubt God, you'll...triumph over huge obstacles. This mountain, for instance, you'll tell, 'Go jump in the lake,' and it will jump. Absolutely everything, ranging from small to large, as you make it a part of your believing prayer, gets included as you lay hold of God."

MATTHEW 21:21–22 MSG

The Inside Rather Than the Outside

God, I remember the story of David. He was the youngest of Jesse's sons, and yet You chose him over the older and bigger ones. You reminded Samuel, whom You had sent to anoint the king, that You look at the inside of a person, not the outside appearance. You saw something in young David's heart, didn't You, Lord? You chose him to do an important job. You selected him as king!

Father, I can relate to David, the shepherd boy whom Jesse had not even bothered to call in from the field. No one imagined David would be the one chosen. No one ever seems to notice me either. It's not that I am disliked exactly...or the least beautiful. I just feel really average sometimes, like there is nothing outstanding about me. The story of David is a great reminder, Lord, that You use regular people—sometimes even those whom no one would suspect—to do special things in Your kingdom! When You look at my heart, I pray that You will find me faithful and ready to serve. Amen.

♥

But the Lord said to Samuel, "Do not consider his appearance or his height, for I have rejected him. The Lord does not look at the things people look at. People look at the outward appearance, but the Lord looks at the heart."
1 Samuel 16:7 niv

Day 146
Loneliness

I know You have promised to never leave me, God, but sometimes I just need a real person to be there for me. All the difficulties of life can pile up until I am totally overwhelmed, and even in the midst of family and friends I feel alone. Like no one can really understand what I am going through, even like no one cares. While my head may tell me that's not true, that's still the way I *feel*.

In Philippians 4:19, Your Word tells me that You will supply everything I need. And in Matthew 6 and Luke 12, it says that You know exactly what I need and will provide it for me. Why is that so hard to grasp? I guess that's where faith and trust come in. Lord, help me keep my focus on You and to believe the truth found in Your Word and not rely on my emotions or feelings.

There *are* people in my life who love me and care about me. You have placed them there because You care for me most of all. When loneliness or circumstances overwhelm me, remind me of Your love for me. Amen.

When I am overwhelmed,
you alone know the way I should turn.
PSALM 142:3 NLT

Day 147
Can't Decide?

Making decisions is hard. Should I try out for the softball team? Should I buy that outfit? Does this hairstyle look good on me? What if I try something new and I fail?

Every morning I rush to get ready for school. Running out the door, I wonder if I'll do well on my tests or if I'll have a good or bad day. I fear that I'll do something stupid or embarrassing today or that someone will do or say something to hurt me. Then I think about how to respond.

The truth is that I don't need to worry about those things or make any decisions on my own. You, my God, greet me each morning with Your love. If I take a few minutes in the morning to pray, You help me through whatever I might have to face and any decisions I need to make.

Help me today, Father. Let Your love guide my path in whatever decisions I face. Show me the way when I'm clueless. I depend on You to help me make the right decisions. Amen.

Remind me each morning of your constant love,
for I put my trust in you. My prayers go up to
you; show me the way I should go.
PSALM 143:8 GNT

A Work in Progress

I mess up a lot, God. I get upset over something small. I tell a lie. I try to live as Your Word instructs, but I find myself giving in to temptations at times. I go my own way and then have to find my way back to You again. You are always there, ready to take me back. I just wish I could stay on track better! It is times like that when I remember that I am simply a work in progress. You aren't finished with me yet!

Just like a sculptor uses his skilled hands to transform a lump of clay into something extraordinary, You are steadily molding me into the woman I will one day become. And even then, I will still be imperfect. You will always be teaching me and perfecting me—until Jesus comes back. Thank You, Father, that it is okay to be imperfect. You have begun something great in me, and I am a wonderful work in progress. I love You, Lord. Amen.

And I am certain that God, who began the good work within you, will continue his work until it is finally finished on the day when Christ Jesus returns.

PHILIPPIANS 1:6 NLT

Day 149
Mouth Guard

I should always have control of my tongue, Jesus, but I don't always think about my words before they pop out of my mouth. But You know that because You hear everything I say—the good *and* the bad. Please forgive me for the times I say things I shouldn't.

I truly want my speech to be honoring to You. Of course, one of those ways is to give Your name the respect it deserves and not misuse it. That's so important, You made it one of Your commandments!

There are other obvious ways words can be used incorrectly: cursing and calling people names. But there are ways that even seem less harmful but can still do a lot of damage: gossiping, speaking in a mean way to siblings, or making fun of someone but passing it off as "a joke."

You made my tongue, heavenly Father, but You made it to honor You and those You have created. Please help me to think about what I say before I say it and to choose only words that will be pure, positive, and encouraging to everyone around me. Amen.

Set a guard, O LORD, over my mouth;
keep watch over the door of my lips!
PSALM 141:3 ESV

Day 150
What a Mess!

Okay, I'll admit it, Lord…sometimes I can be a little messy. My space gets cluttered. Dirty clothes cover the floor. I can't always find my school supplies or all the pieces to my games. I'm not thrilled when my parents ask me to clean up. Seems pointless. After all, it will just get messy again tomorrow! So I don't always do the best job, to be honest.

Then I hear stories of kids who have no games, very few clothes, and no school supplies. What they do have, they take excellent care of. When I hear these stories, I'm ashamed of my messy room. If cleanliness matters to You, God, it should matter to me too. Help me to do the very best with the things that have been given to me. I know this brings honor to You! Amen.

Even small children are known by their actions,
so is their conduct really pure and upright?
PROVERBS 20:11 NIV

Day 151
Comfort from God

Heavenly Father, sometimes I find it hard to feel comforted by You because You can't physically give me a hug and I haven't heard the actual sound of Your voice. But one of the ways that You do comfort is by providing people who love me and can hug me and listen to me and speak words of wisdom into my life. Thank You for providing me with those people and for being there for me, even if I can't actually see You. Help me to feel Your presence in my heart, even if I can't see You with my eyes. I want to be comforted by Your scripture and by being able to talk to You; remind me of these things when I'm feeling lonely or depressed. I know that all comfort and all love come from You. I just forget that sometimes. Help me to always remember Your love and Your comfort are in my heart. Amen.

Show me a sign of your goodness.
When my enemies look, they will be ashamed.
You, LORD, have helped me and comforted me.
PSALM 86:17 NCV

The Ups and Downs of Friendship

Thank You for my many friends, heavenly Father. Some I've had for a long time, and other friendships have developed more recently. There are those I can hang out with and others I can trust with my deepest secrets, hopes, and dreams.

Some friends have (and more will!) let me down. Help me to be quick to forgive them when that happens. I pray that I won't let others down, but, if I do, that I will be quick to ask for forgiveness and make the relationship right again. I want to be a good friend—one who is trustworthy, loyal, reliable, and compassionate. Please don't let me give anyone a reason to ever regret calling me "friend."

I ask for wisdom in choosing my friends. I ask that You guide me to the ones who will be a good influence and will encourage me in my walk with You.

Thank You for being the most perfect friend anyone could ever have. You're never too busy to listen, and You will always make decisions based on what is best for me, whether I like it or not. There is no better friend than You! Amen.

Friends come and friends go,
but a true friend sticks by you like family.
PROVERBS 18:24 MSG

Day 153
Imperfection and Airbrushing

Dear God, my face is absolutely a mess today. I just don't understand how it always seems to happen overnight and usually before an important event too. I know they say that blemishes on the face are worse during adolescence and that it will get better, but right now it seems hopeless. I'd love to have a complexion like the magazine cover girls, but then they say even the models don't look that good in person. Still, it would be wonderful to be able to airbrush my face in real life.

So here I am in front of the mirror again hoping that I'll see something miraculous take place and suddenly the pimples will be gone and I'll have beautiful, clear skin. But I know that's not going to happen. Everything in this world is imperfect, and I guess that includes our bodies doing weird things while we're growing up.

So I have to just make the best of it. Thank You that someone invented Clearasil and Proactiv and all those special soaps and creams. At least I live in a century where there is some help! So I'll cover what I can and then ask You to shine through me because that's what matters most anyway. Amen.

I will praise the LORD at all times.
PSALM 34:1 NLT

The Present Moment

Sometimes, Father, I want to be so grown up. I want to make decisions on my own, do what I want to do when I want to do it. Then at other times, I'm so glad I'm not yet an adult. Older people seem to have so many responsibilities—ones I'm definitely not ready for.

Help me to be happy in the present moment, Lord. To live for today and not worry about tomorrow. Remind me that every day with You is a good day.

Give me the strength to be patient and the wisdom to know what is good for me at whatever age I am. Help me to respect and obey my parents, teachers, and other trustworthy adults. After all, You have put them in my life for a reason—to protect, teach, and care for me until I am ready and grown up enough to take care of myself.

So I will be content, learning from others and waiting for You to grow me up into the person You have planned me to be. Thank You, Lord, for being with me every stage of my life, gently leading me, tenderly supporting me, and blessing me day after day. Amen.

This is the day the LORD has made;
we will rejoice and be glad in it.
PSALM 118:24 NKJV

Day 155
God Holds Me Up

Fear. Anxiety. Feeling alone. Looking all around for a friend, someone to help me, someone who cares and understands. . . These are all things I experience, Lord. What a wonderful promise I have in Your Word that You are my God. You tell me that You are with me and that I do not ever need to be afraid or worried. You promise to help, to give me strength, and to hold me up. Does it get any better than that? The Almighty God of the universe is going to hold me up!

I think about when I was just a very little girl and how I would ride on the shoulders of a big strong man and feel that I was secure. I was lifted up above it all. I was the "princess." Thank You, Lord, that because of my faith in Jesus, I am Your daughter. I am a treasured daughter of the King of kings, loved and protected by none other than You! I pray that all the days of my life I will remember that I am never alone. I always have my God. Amen.

"Do not fear, for I am with you; do not be afraid,
for I am your God. I will strengthen you, I will
also help you, I will also uphold you
with My righteous right hand."
ISAIAH 41:10 NASB

Endurance

Some days just aren't that great. Life gets hard, and I get tired. But the last thing I want to do is give up. God, I need Your help in going forward, in keeping on. They say "life is a journey," but sometimes it just feels like a wild ride and I'm doing my best just to hang on!

The dictionary defines endurance as "the ability to withstand hardship or adversity." I don't want to be beaten down by life or the things that happen to me. I want to be the best I can be, to win the prize, to reach the goal. This verse in Hebrews tells me I can do that by keeping my eyes on Jesus. He endured so much for me.

God, help me to look to Jesus as my example. Give me the strength I need to continue on. Amen.

Let us strip off every weight that slows us down, especially the sin that so easily trips us up. And let us run with endurance the race God has set before us. We do this by keeping our eyes on Jesus, the champion who initiates and perfects our faith. Because of the joy awaiting him, he endured the cross, disregarding its shame. Now he is seated in the place of honor beside God's throne.

HEBREWS 12:1–2 NLT

A Giving Heart

Dear God, I have a desire to be genuinely kind to people. Not just my family and friends—everyone! The cashier at my favorite ice cream shop, the librarian at school, and even kids I don't know. Some people are much easier to love than others, and when it's hard to love someone, I need You to show me how. Show me how to be kind when others aren't kind to me, and give me patience with myself when I mess up. I want kindness to be something that I am known for, especially with my friends when they are going through a hard time and need a listening ear. I want to be a genuine friend, one who is there during the good times and the bad. Please help my thoughts, words, and actions reflect kindness and love to everyone that I meet, and help me to be kind and loyal to my friends. Amen.

Never let loyalty and kindness leave you!
Tie them around your neck as a reminder.
Write them deep within your heart.
PROVERBS 3:3 NLT

Day 158
Worry

Sometimes my thoughts swirl faster than my mind can keep up with. I think about the future and all the what-ifs, what I hope will happen, and what might not. I look at every angle of a problem that could happen, wanting to be prepared "just in case." I plan what to do with money I don't yet have and try to figure out the best way to acquire what I will need to get what I desire. All these things can consume my time—and my peace of mind!

When I struggle with wanting and not having or wondering if something will or won't happen, I need to get off the spinning merry-go-round of emotion and trust You, God, to give me what I need. In Luke 12:29–31 (MSG), Jesus says to "not be so preoccupied with *getting* so you can respond to God's *giving*." It says that those who worry and are preoccupied don't know God or the way He does things. Jesus says that God will meet our human concerns.

I don't want to worry myself into missing what I have, Lord. Help me to trust in You for everything I need. Amen.

Give your burdens to the LORD, and he will take care of you. He will not permit the godly to slip and fall.
PSALM 55:22 NLT

What Is My Purpose?

I look around at all my friends, Lord, and it seems as if they all have a purpose. They have goals—some of them even already know where they want to go to college or what career they want. Some days, I don't even really know what I'm doing or why I'm here. What is *my* purpose, God?

I know from Your Word that You have a plan for everyone who loves You. . .and because *I* love You, I guess that includes me. But I don't know what Your plans are. It would be great if You'd just write them on my ceiling, but then I wouldn't have to trust You as much. And I do want to learn to trust You more.

Show me ways I can use my talents for You, Father. And please help me to be patient as I try to figure out my purpose. It might be months or years until I know what You want me to do, but I will continue following You, trusting You every step of the way.

For we are his workmanship, created in Christ Jesus for good works, which God prepared beforehand, that we should walk in them.
EPHESIANS 2:10 ESV

Day 160
Resting in You

I get so tired sometimes, Lord. Still, I keep going and going and going. It's hard to get out of bed in the morning. Sometimes I just want to keep on sleeping all day long. But I must get up and go, go, go! Seems like I never stop. School. Family. Church. Sports. Homework. Go, go, go.

Your Word says that I should stop, that taking a rest—a break—is a good idea. Even You took a break when You were creating the world, Father! I need to learn from You! If resting was important to You, it should be important to me too.

Do I need to take a break from any activities in my life? If so, show me which ones! In the meantime, I pray that You will give me energy to get through the things I must do. The Bible says that You will give strength to those who are tired. I get really tired sometimes, so I could use a double dose of Your strength! Amen.

He gives strength to the weary and increases the power of the weak. Even youths grow tired and weary, and young men stumble and fall; but those who hope in the LORD will renew their strength.
ISAIAH 40:29–31 NIV

Day 161
Choosing Joy

Dear Lord, whenever I'm down or going through a hard time, give me joy. I know that I focus much more on being happy, but I should focus more on joy because it has a more lasting effect. It's a choice to be joyful, especially during the difficult times. Having joy isn't based on what's going on around me; having joy is an attitude and something that I choose to have. I think that finding joy means focusing on the little blessings that You give me every day, like a beautiful sunset, or time with friends, or making someone else smile. Help me always choose joy and to spread joy to the lives of those around me. And thank You for the happy times, when I don't even have to make a conscious decision to be joyful; it just comes naturally from what is surrounding me. Happy times make it easier to go through difficult times, and for that I am very thankful. Amen.

You make known to me the path of life;
you will fill me with joy in your presence,
with eternal pleasures at your right hand.
PSALM 16:11 NIV

Day 162
Healing Words

Why can't I control my mouth, Lord? Every single day, I say words I wish I could slurp back in. I sass my parents. I say something mean to my brother or sister. I'm sarcastic to my friends. Before I know it, everyone is mad at me and it's my own fault. I wish I could have a REWIND and DELETE button for the things I say.

But no matter how hard I try, I keep messing up. The words just spill out before I realize what I'm saying. I need to learn to think before I speak and choose my words more carefully.

When it comes to my words, I want to be in the construction business, not the demolition business. I want to build people up, not tear them down. I want to be the kind of person whose words bring healing and hope, not heartache and hurt. Help me to edit my words while they're still in my head, before they come out of my mouth. I want to honor You and share Your love, Lord, with everything I say. Amen.

The words of the reckless pierce like swords,
but the tongue of the wise brings healing.
PROVERBS 12:18 NIV

Happy in Hoping

I have hope, heavenly Father! I'm so thankful that I don't have to base my happiness on things around me, because life is pretty stressful sometimes even for a girl my age.

When I was little, it didn't take much to make me happy—a new toy or book or a trip to McDonald's. But now I know that life isn't always fixed easily; there aren't any Band-Aids for divorce and cancer and friends who move away. Life can really hurt! But I'm glad I know about You and the purpose my relationship with You brings to my life. No matter how bad things get, I know there is always hope because You promised You'd never leave me and that someday I'll live with You.

Sometimes I overhear others talking about the bad things happening in their lives, and they seem to have no hope at all. What a terrible feeling that must be! Help me to share with them the solid hope I have because of You and the strength that gives me to get up each morning and know I can make it with Your help. I love You, Jesus! Amen.

Blessed are those whose help is the God of Jacob,
whose hope is in the LORD their God.
PSALM 146:5 NIV

Day 164
Seen but Not Heard

Lord, because I am young, there are times when I feel I am being seen but my voice is not being heard. I'm tired of adults not listening to what I have to say. But perhaps it is how I am expressing myself.

Help me, Lord, to be an example to others—even grown-ups! Give me the patience to think before I speak. And then give me the right words to say—or not say—at the right time. Give me the heart to love everyone, to be gentle, kind, and respectful. Boost up my faith so that I can have confidence in myself and, even more importantly, in You. Help me to stay pure in thought, word, and deed by giving me the courage to say no when I need to.

I am trusting You, Lord, to set me on the right path in all situations. I am counting on You to eventually make me into the woman You know I can be. I leave it all in Your hands, knowing You'll make all things beautiful in their time—including me!

Let no one despise or think less of you because of your youth, but be an example (pattern) for the believers in speech, in conduct, in love, in faith, and in purity.
1 TIMOTHY 4:12 AMPC

Day 165
A Choice to Make

Father, I know that I have a choice to make. It seems like I am faced with it every single day. I must choose whether to follow the world or to travel the narrow road with You. The road to popularity is not the right road for a believer in Christ. My values and attitudes just don't match up with those who do not know You. Your disciples faced this challenge. I read about it in Your Word.

Things are no different today. What the world says is cool is often the direct opposite of Your commands. I know that Your guidelines for my life are set with my best interest in mind. You are not trying to keep me from anything that is good. You want only the very best for me. Every perfect gift comes from You, my heavenly Father. When You look at my heart, I pray that You are pleased. I will always choose You over this world. Give me the strength, wisdom, and endurance I will need as I continue to walk with You. Amen.

He said to them, "You are the ones who justify yourselves in the eyes of others, but God knows your hearts. What people value highly is detestable in God's sight."
LUKE 16:15 NIV

Giving Till It Hurts

I've never thought of myself as stingy, Lord, but sometimes it does hurt to give to others. Time, money, things—in every relationship it all costs me something. Yet Your Word tells me that when I give I will receive. Whatever I give out will come flowing back in full measure and overflowing.

Jesus' words in Luke chapter 6 say that the measure I use to give to others will be the same measure used to give to me. That's a pretty good return! The funny part is, even though it may be painful at first to give up something that I want for myself and give it to others, in the end I get more benefit than they do!

God, help me to continue to think of others before myself and to be willing to give without hesitation. I will trust You to bring back to me all I need in the same way I have given to others. Amen.

"Give, and you will receive. You will be given much. Pressed down, shaken together, and running over, it will spill into your lap. The way you give to others is the way God will give to you."
LUKE 6:38 NCV

Day 167
Just Ask

When I ask my parents for something, they sometimes say "yes," "no," "wait," or "we'll see."

Thank You for my parents; I know they love me and want what's best for me. But sometimes they refuse my requests, though I don't fully understand why. I guess that's when I just have to trust their judgment.

Jesus, You said that when I ask, I'll receive. I know that doesn't mean You'll always say yes; rather, You *will* answer my prayers. Help me to seek You more through prayer. I believe that You never turn from anyone who comes to You with an open, sincere heart. I open my heart to You now, Lord. I seek Your will for my life and ask that You give me wisdom, strength, direction, and guidance. Sometimes You do that through my parents, so I ask that You help me obey and listen to them as I should. Other times, You direct me through Your gentle, quiet voice within or through the godly advice of a teacher or grandparent.

Thank You for listening to my prayers and answering! Even when the answer is "no" or "we'll see." Amen.

"Ask, and you will receive; seek, and you will find; knock, and the door will be opened to you."
MATTHEW 7:7 GNT

Day 168
The Talk

Dear God, it seems so easy to get caught up in talking about other people behind their backs. So many of my friends do it, and it's hard not to join in sometimes. Please forgive me for being a part of that, and help me to change.

Please give me fresh ideas and topics to talk about with my friends so I don't get sucked into talking about other people in negative ways. And when one of my friends begins to talk about someone else in a way that makes me uncomfortable or doesn't sound very kind, help me to say something nice about that person and quickly change the subject. Or if it continues and my friends just won't stop, please give me the courage to leave, even if my friends will get mad.

I want the words of my mouth to be pleasing to You, Jesus (Psalm 19:14). Help me to choose good friends who talk kindly about others. Help me not to be naive either. If my friends talk about other people behind their back, they are probably talking about me too. Amen.

It is foolish to belittle one's neighbor;
a sensible person keeps quiet. A gossip goes
around telling secrets, but those who are
trustworthy can keep a confidence.
PROVERBS 11:12–13 NLT

Wonderfully Made

Your Word tells me that I am wonderfully made. I want to remember that, Lord, when the world—through people and media—tell me differently. Psalm 139 talks about how You made and formed me and that every day of my life was recorded in Your book before I was even born! You think about me all the time. You like how I look—You made me that way!

I know that being healthy and caring for my physical body is important, but sometimes I feel like I am on a treadmill going nowhere. I don't want to be dissatisfied with who I am—especially about the things I can't change. There are times when I need a new perspective. I am thankful that when I look at myself through Your eyes, I see a different kind of person than what the world might see.

Help me to *like* who I am, God, and to remember that I am *me*—the me You made me to be! Help me not only to remember that but to embrace it as well. Amen.

You made all the delicate, inner parts of my
body and knit me together in my mother's womb.
Thank you for making me so wonderfully complex!
Your workmanship is marvelous—how well I know it.
PSALM 139:13–14 NLT

Day 170
A Volcano of Anger

Temper, temper! Father, sometimes I let mine get the best of me. I feel like a volcano is stirring up inside of me and then. . .*bam*! I blow! What a mess. My anger never solves the problem. In fact, it always makes things worse.

You tell me in Your Word that I shouldn't let my anger reach the boiling point. I should be quick to listen and slow to speak. And when I do speak, my words shouldn't be angry or demanding!

Getting in arguments isn't a good thing. Blowing up at people isn't either! You want me to be kind to everyone. I can't do that as long as I have anger in my heart. So I ask You to remove my temper today. Take it away, Lord. Calm me down and show me how to react the way You would react. . .even when I'm upset. I trust You, Lord. Amen.

A servant of the Lord must not quarrel but must be kind to everyone, be able to teach, and be patient with difficult people.
2 TIMOTHY 2:24 NLT

Day 171
Honest Words

Lord, it's so easy to lie sometimes and make things easier for myself. But guilt usually overwhelms me after I lie, and I know that I've done something wrong. When I'm tempted to lie to get out of trouble or to be polite, remind me how honesty is important. I want my family and friends to be able to trust what I say; I want to be known for honesty in every area of my life. Even a "polite" lie is wrong, so help me to be gentle when someone asks my opinion on something and I answer them with honesty. And help me to be honest with myself and with You, Lord. I know that You will never judge me for the thoughts or feelings that I have, but I sometimes judge myself or lie to myself about things. I need Your help to be completely honest with myself and see all of my faults, not hide them or refuse to acknowledge that they are there. Give me the grace to be honest with myself and others when I've messed up and done something wrong. Amen.

If you do the right thing, honesty will be your guide. But if you are crooked, you will be trapped by your own dishonesty.
PROVERBS 11:3 CEV

Day 172
Let Somebody Else

I'm good at a lot of things, Lord. I have many things I like to do, many things I do well. The problem is, not everyone knows about all the things I'm good at. Sometimes other people get recognized for things, and I get ignored. That's not fun.

That's when I open my big mouth and start telling people all the things I'm good at. I want people to be impressed with me. I want everyone to know what a cool, talented, amazing girl I am.

But when I tell people about all my great gifts, no one seems impressed. That's when I realize. . .I was bragging. Oops. I don't want to come across as a brag.

Help me remember that no matter how hard it is to feel passed over and ignored, it's usually best to stay quiet about my own strengths. I should do my best in everything and let others figure out what I'm good at. Praise always feels better when it comes from someone else and not from my own mouth.

Remind me of that today, Lord. Amen.

Let someone else praise you, and not your own mouth; an outsider, and not your own lips.
PROVERBS 27:2 NIV

Day 173
Guilty Feelings

Dear God, I feel guilty today. I've done something that is wrong, and I feel terribly dirty inside. I knew I shouldn't have done it, but I did it anyway. I didn't listen to the voice of Your Holy Spirit warning me. I just jumped in and did it.

Now, I feel so sorry, but I can't get rid of this feeling that I'm in the shadows and there's no way out. I'd like to jump in a car wash or maybe Niagara Falls and get rid of the icky feeling down inside. I wish so badly that I had resisted temptation and said no.

I know that You are a God of mercy and forgiveness, so I'm coming to You right now and asking You to make me clean. I've sinned, and I know it. Please forgive me and restore me in Your sight, and let me be wiser and on my guard against temptation.

I'm glad that Jesus died for my sins and that You are ready to forgive when I ask. Thank You for loving me always. In Jesus' name, amen.

If we confess our sins, He is faithful and just
to forgive us our sins and to cleanse
us from all unrighteousness.
1 John 1:9 nkjv

All That Really Matters

Lord, sometimes I feel so different from other kids because I go to church and try to follow You. Yet deep in my heart, I know that You are real and that I am on the right path.

So, Father, help me to put aside the people who put me down because I am a Christian. And, Lord, pull me closer to You and Your church.

Please show me how I can serve You, how I can show Your love to everyone I meet, how I can follow Your commandment to love You with all my heart, soul, and mind and to love others as I love myself. For when I really think about it, loving You and others is all that really matters in this world. Yet sometimes that's not easy. So I really need Your strength—each and every moment of the day. Give me the peace that comes from following You. And help me to encourage others as You encourage me. In Jesus' name I pray, amen.

Some people have gotten out of the habit of meeting for worship, but we must not do that. We should keep on encouraging each other, especially since you know that the day of the Lord's coming is getting closer.
HEBREWS 10:25 CEV

Day 175
Light in the Darkness

I remember as a little girl being so afraid of the dark. I always wanted my parents to leave a night-light on or the door to my bedroom cracked open at night. There was just something frightening about not being able to see in the darkness! I have to admit, Father, the darkness still scares me. Not literal darkness. . .but the darkness of the world. There is so much evil out there, God. I hear things that frighten me—news reports of unspeakable murders and other crimes. Sometimes even more frightening is the darkness that I see even in my own school and neighborhood. I know kids who disobey their parents and do things that are very wrong.

Help me, Lord, when I am in the midst of evil, to remember what You have taught me in the light. You are always with me, and I can always call on You to shine Your light into the darkness and show me the way to go. I trust You, Lord. Lead me through this dark world on a path filled with Your glorious light. Amen.

If I say, "Surely the darkness will hide me and the light become night around me," even the darkness will not be dark to you; the night will shine like the day, for darkness is as light to you.
PSALM 139:11–12 NIV

Thoughts about Science Class

Well, Father, we're talking about the "E" word now. That's right—evolution, the origin of the earth and mankind and the development of the species. I have to admit that some of it sounds pretty convincing, but I can't forget that the Bible says You created the world and everything in it.

Many scientists think this evolution thing is true, that the earth really is millions of years old and that we all came from a single cell in the water somewhere. I'm glad, God, for all those Sunday school lessons about creation. I'm glad I don't have to believe I am the product of some random process. I'm happy that I know You created this world and me with a purpose.

I know I can't convince all my friends that Creation is the right view, but help me be true to the truth when I am asked. I don't want to cave in because I'm afraid to be different. Thank You that I know the truth and the real science always agrees with it. Amen.

For in six days the LORD made the heavens and the earth, the sea, and all that is in them.
EXODUS 20:11 NKJV

Thank You for Loving Me

I love so many people and things: my parents and family; my pet; my friends; favorite teachers; swimming in the summertime; eating chocolate ice cream; and most of all, You, Lord.

It's hard for me to realize that You love me even when I don't deserve it. You are perfect in every way, and I am so imperfect! Yet Your love is constant and lasting. Friends come and go, but You remain faithful no matter what I do or don't do. How can that be?

Thank You that no matter how unlovable I am on certain days, You still keep on loving me! When I feel so unlovable and undeserving, You remind me that Your love extends far beyond what I could ever imagine. That's amazing!

I'm so blessed because even when I deserve Your anger, You keep on loving me. You accept me as I am; You forgive my sins and cleanse my heart. I love You, Lord. Thank You for loving me so much. Amen.

♥

God is sheer mercy and grace; not easily angered, he's rich in love. He doesn't endlessly nag and scold, nor hold grudges forever. He doesn't treat us as our sins deserve, nor pay us back in full for our wrongs. As high as heaven is over the earth, so strong is his love to those who fear him.
Psalm 103:8–10 msg

Day 178
Choose Life

I choose life, Lord. I want to love You with all that I am. I want to obey Your words. And I want to stay close to You all of my life. Your Word tells me that eternal life is knowing You through Your Son, Jesus Christ (John 17:3) and that You came to give me abundant life (John 10:10)—even here, right now on this earth, as I wait to be with You forever in heaven.

Help me to remember that during hard days at school—and especially when my friends seem to forget all about You. Please stay close to my heart always. Allow me to speak up for You in situations where You are forgotten and overlooked. Let my life be a reminder to everyone around me that You are alive and well and still working in the hearts and minds of those who seek after You.

Thank You for giving me life, Jesus. I praise Your name! Amen.

I am offering you life or death, blessings or curses.
Now, choose life! Then you and your children
may live. To choose life is to love the LORD
your God, obey him, and stay close to him.
DEUTERONOMY 30:19–20 NCV

Day 179
Forgive Them?

You really expect me to *forgive* them, Jesus? After what they did to me? I can usually let a lot of things go, but not this time. This time, it hurts too much.

Father, that person who I thought was my friend just hurt me, and the pain feels like it's more than I can handle. How could they do that to me? I wish You knew what it felt like. . .then You'd understand.

Oh. . .but You do understand what it's like. Your friend took a bribe to turn You in when You hadn't done anything wrong. You were humiliated. You were made fun of and tortured. And You were killed in a cruel way. But some of Your last words were ones of forgiveness. How was that possible? The people who hurt You didn't even apologize. . .but You still forgave them anyway.

And Jesus, I have hurt You with my sin, but You keep forgiving me anyway. Father, please give me the strength to be like You. Help me to forgive, whether I receive an apology or not. In Jesus' name, amen.

♥

Be kind to one another, tenderhearted,
forgiving one another, as God in Christ forgave you.

EPHESIANS 4:32 ESV

Day 180
Self-Discipline

Lord, I have to admit, it's not always easy to do everything I'm told. When my parents give me instructions, I should follow them, but sometimes I slack off. I get busy doing other things and forget. Unless they remind me, I don't always get things done. Then my parents discipline me. Embarrassing!

The Bible says that You can give me self-discipline. That means I shouldn't have to wait on others to remind me to do things like clean my room, put dishes away, or do my homework. I shouldn't have to wait for my teacher to say, "Did you finish that project I gave you to do?" With Your help, Father, I can do those things on my own, without being reminded over and over again.

Please teach me how to be self-disciplined, Lord. Can You remind me to take care of things and show me how to be responsible? I want to grow up to be the very best me I can possibly be! With Your help, I know I can do it! Amen.

For the Spirit God gave us does not make us timid, but gives us power, love and self-discipline.
2 TIMOTHY 1:7 NIV

Day 181
When I Feel Insecure

Heavenly Father, I feel so insecure sometimes. I feel insecure about what others think of me, how I look or dress, whether or not anyone actually likes me. It is just the worst feeling whenever these thoughts come over me. I don't want to feel this way, and I don't always know what to do when this happens. Whenever I'm feeling insecure, help me to remember to turn to You and look to You for the security that I need. Nothing else will bring lasting security, no matter how hard I try or who I listen to—only true peace of mind will come from You. Help me base who I am in You, not in the things I do, how I look, or whom I hang out with. I know that I am Your child—remind me of that when I feel like no one loves me or wants to be around me. Thank You for Your constant love and security, heavenly Father. Amen.

Only God can save me, and I calmly wait for him.
God alone is the mighty rock that keeps me
safe and the fortress where I am secure.
PSALM 62:1–2 CEV

Day 182
Avoid Gossip

Why do my friends talk about each other, Lord? And it's not just my friends. I do it too. For some reason, whenever two or more of us get together, we often end up saying mean things about someone who isn't there to defend herself. I don't know why we do it. But in the moment, gossip is hard to resist.

I don't want to be a gossip, Lord. I've been hurt by gossip, and I don't want my words to hurt other people. And I've heard that those who gossip about others to me will probably gossip about me to others.

I want to be accepted. I want to be part of the group. A lot of times the best way to be part of the group is to join in their mean talk. Many times I find myself sharing personal things about my own life with these mean-spirited people in hopes that they'll accept me as one of them.

Help me to be kind in my words about others and wise in what I share about myself. And help me find friends who want to be kind and wise too. Amen.

A gossip betrays a confidence;
so avoid anyone who talks too much.
PROVERBS 20:19 NIV

Crowning Glory...or Not!

My hair doesn't like to cooperate with me, Lord. When I'm getting ready to go somewhere, it just refuses to look like I want it to.

I know there are more important matters than hairstyle, but it seems really big to me. At times I just want to sit down and cry, but that wouldn't help anything. So instead I mutter and yank and go out the door feeling terribly ugly.

I hope other people don't think my hair looks as bad as I think it does. I just wish I could go somewhere and hide until I know how to get it right. I feel stupid when I can't even get my hair to look nice.

But thank You, God, that You don't love me for my hair. After all, You saw me before I was born when I didn't have any hair at all! And You've loved me from the beginning of time.

So please help me to do the best I can and believe that I will get better with practice. I'll probably still have bad hair days once in a while, but I don't have to judge my life by them. Amen.

But the very hairs of your head are all numbered.
MATTHEW 10:30 KJV

Day 184
In God's Grip

Father God, many days my courage and my strength are tested. I'm wondering if I'm making the right decisions—from which subjects to study to which friends to hang out with. I want to do the right thing and to have people like me too, but I also want to be true to You—and to myself. That's when fear and confusion begin to creep in.

Then, just when I feel myself beginning to panic, I remember that not only are You *with* me in every situation I face, but You are also going *before* me, clearing the way. So I need not give in to fear. I can have confidence that You are holding on to my hand. You have me in Your grip. And You are so much more powerful than any problems this world can bring.

Help me walk *Your* way with the courage You provide twenty-four hours a day. Keep reminding me that You will never let me down but will raise me up to face any challenges that come my way. Thank You for keeping me in Your grip.

"Be strong. Take courage. Don't be intimidated.
Don't give them a second thought because God,
your God, is striding ahead of you. He's right there
with you. He won't let you down; he won't leave you."
DEUTERONOMY 31:6 MSG

Humility

It seems like I am in competition for everything, Lord. There are opportunities at school such as the spelling bee, student council positions, citizenship awards, and honor society. I feel like we are all seeking to climb to the top. Even when the teacher pairs us up to work on projects, I find myself wanting to be with someone who is popular, smart, and attractive rather than that quiet kid whom no one notices.

Help me to remember that none of my goals can be met on my own. I need Your help. And when I am in leadership roles or win an award of any kind, I want to always remember to give You the glory. I will serve as a leader at my school or church or in any situation You see fit. But even if I rise to the top, let me always remember You are above me. I am Your humble servant. Use me as You will. And give me opportunities to build others up. I don't want to be jealous if someone outshines me. Envy is never a good feeling! Help me to always choose humility. Amen.

Whoever is the greatest should be the servant of the others. If you put yourself above others, you will be put down. But if you humble yourself, you will be honored.
MATTHEW 23:11–12 CEV

Day 186
Words Can Hurt You

"Sticks and stones may break my bones, but words can never hurt me." Not true! Words have the power to cause great pain. They can slice and wound so deep that healing from them may seem impossible. I've seen it happen—relationships that are never the same after careless words are spoken.

God, please help me guard my mouth so that I never hurt others as I have been hurt by thoughtless words. Proverbs 25:11 (NCV) says, "The right word spoken at the right time is as beautiful as gold apples in a silver bowl." Let my words encourage others and not tear them down.

Even in joking around, words can hurt. I don't like to be teased about certain things, and it's not always easy to know what might bother others. I like making others laugh, but it should never be at another person's expense. Help me be kind to others, and when they are unkind to me, help me to forgive them.

Help me respond to those around me in a way that is honoring to them—and to You, God. Amen.

♥

Just as damaging as a madman shooting a deadly
weapon is someone who lies to a friend
and then says, "I was only joking."
PROVERBS 26:18–19 NLT

Why Worry? Pray!

Should I let my hair grow long? Am I pretty enough?
Will I make the team? Is my friend still angry with me?
Did I get a good grade on my history quiz?

Father, I worry about a lot of things. Each day gives
me something new to worry about! I just can't seem
to help myself. Yet You tell Your children not to worry
and to pray instead. I need help with that, Lord. My
first reaction is to fret rather than pray. I know You care
about me and the things I care about. So remind me
of that when my own thoughts cause me such unrest
and conflict.

Father, I give You all of my worries right now and
ask that You help me sort through them. Please give
me the answers I need and the peace that comes with
surrendering my problems and concerns to You. Thank
You, Lord. Amen.

Don't worry about anything; instead, pray about
everything. Tell God what you need, and thank
him for all he has done. Then you will
experience God's peace.
PHILIPPIANS 4:6–7 NLT

A Measure of Love

Heavenly Father, help me not to look down on other people, thinking that I'm better than they are. That is pride, and I know You oppose the proud just like it says in James 4:6. It also tells me that You show favor to the humble. I certainly don't want You to be against me, Lord. That would be terrifying and lonely. I pray for Your favor on my life and the plans that You help me make.

Help me not to condemn and judge other people when I have no right to do that. I'm not You. But when a friend of mine is choosing sin over Your plan, help me be able to talk to her out of love and friendship instead of acting like I know it all and that I have everything figured out. Give me wisdom to confront the friends that I feel You nudging me to talk to. But help me always to do it in love—with a clean heart before You. Amen.

"For in the same way you judge others, you will be judged, and with the measure you use, it will be measured to you."
MATTHEW 7:2 NIV

Living without Regrets

Heavenly Father, I'm struggling with guilt from a bad choice. It feels like it's strapped to my back, and I'll need to carry it every day for the rest of my life.

I feel like I need to keep saying I'm sorry. Maybe that will make it feel better. Or maybe I need to do a lot of good things to make up for it. Then I will make up for that mistake, right?

No, Your Word tells me that if I say I'm sorry for my sin, You will take it away. But not only that, You choose to forget about it! How can You do that when I can't? But Your promises are true, so if that's what You say, then I can believe it.

Your Word also tells me that I don't need to try to do a lot of good things to make up for my sin. I only need to tell You I'm sorry. It all sounds too easy for the amount of guilt I've been carrying around.

Lord Jesus, I ask for Your forgiveness for what I've done. Help me trust that You forgive me and won't hold my sin against me. Thank You, Father! In Jesus' name, amen.

"For I will forgive their wickedness and will remember their sins no more."
HEBREWS 8:12 NIV

What's Happening Tomorrow?

Sometimes I wish I could see into the future, Lord! I wish I knew what I was going to be when I'm all grown up. Will I be a doctor who cures people of their illnesses? A teacher who helps her students learn and grow? A gymnast who competes in the Olympics? A missionary in some foreign land? A mom who loves and plays with her kids? Ooo, I can hardly wait. But I have no choice. One day I'll know the answer to that question, but in the meantime, please help me with all of the changes I'm going through—in my body, my mind, and my heart. Seems like every day I'm changing a little more. Guess that's part of "growing up."

Everyone goes through changes, so I know I'm not the only one. And I'm sure everyone gets a little scared about the future. Remind me that You've got this, Lord! You will direct my path and will give me wisdom as I go through changes, large or small! Amen.

♥

Trust in the Lord with all your heart and lean not on your own understanding; in all your ways submit to him, and he will make your paths straight.

PROVERBS 3:5–6 NIV

Popularity

God, I really want people to like me and want to be around me. I want to be popular in school and have people think I'm awesome. I know that everyone has these desires, but that doesn't make them any less hard to deal with. Sometimes I find myself changing what I like or who I hang out with based on what other people think. I don't want to do things like that. I know that changing myself isn't a good way to be happy and content. When I'm in a situation where I feel pressure to do things because they are "cool," help me to stop and think about what I'm doing and not give in to the pressure of my peers. Help me to stand up for what I believe and show others that I believe in You and want to glorify You with my words and actions. The main goal in my life shouldn't be popularity, and sometimes I forget that. Please help me to remember, and be patient with me when I mess up. Amen.

So with God and Christ as witnesses, I command you to preach God's message. Do it willingly, even if it isn't the popular thing to do.
2 TIMOTHY 4:1–2 CEV

Day 192
Quiet Time

Dear God, I really struggle to make time for You in my life. I want to daily set aside time to spend talking with You and reading Your words. It is so easy for me to spend time with my friends or to do fun things, and when I'm in a rush or stressed, time with You is the first thing that I give up. Help me to be faithful in spending time with You regularly, building my relationship with You, and not just when I need Your help. When things are going well in my life, I tend to forget that You want my company and want me to talk to You. But the second that things get hard, You are the first person I want to talk to and share my problems with. Help me to remember that You are more than just a "fixer" and that I should talk to You about all the good things in my life, not just the bad. Amen.

I thirst for the living God.
When can I go to meet with him?
PSALM 42:2 NCV

Praying for My Prince

God, I want to get married someday to the man of my dreams. I know that not everyone gets married, but I hope it's in Your plan for me. I have a lot of things on my list that I'd like to have in a future husband, but I want You to have the final say.

Of course, I'd like to have a handsome husband, one who is tall and strong and nice to look at, and I'd like for him to treat me with respect and really be in love with me. But I suppose that first I should look for a man who has given his heart and life to You; that kind of guy will have the motivation to love me as he should.

Today, I pray for the man who will someday be my husband. Give his parents wisdom to train him right, give him a pastor who will preach truth to him, and give him a heart that wants to follow You. Protect him from Satan's plans and help him to keep his mind and body pure. Bring us together in Your timing and bless our lives together. In Jesus' name, amen.

For everything there is a season. . .
a time to love. . .
ECCLESIASTES 3:1, 8 NLT

A Purpose and a Plan

Disappointment? I know it only too well. From not getting what I wanted for my birthday, to not getting picked for the team, to having someone I thought was my friend betray me, to losing a game.

When disappointment comes, I find myself getting grouchy, saying mean things, or pouting. But, strangely enough, behaving that way doesn't make me feel any better. In fact, it makes me feel worse.

Your Word says that You, Lord, are working out for my good everything that happens in my life. You have a plan for me. And there's a purpose to that plan. So help me to let disappointment and discouragement roll off me like water off a duck's back. Help me to just shrug it off when things don't go my way. Help me to look on the bright side, seeing Your hand and Your heart in my life, knowing that, like my parents, You know and want what's best for me—You have a better way. Amen.

We are assured and know that [God being a partner in their labor] all things work together and are [fitting into a plan] for good to and for those who love God and are called according to [His] design and purpose.

ROMANS 8:28 AMPC

Day 195
An Example

I am just a kid still, God. There are so many things I can't do—like driving or dating! There are lots of things I can't control—such as where I attend school or even what I have for dinner! But You tell me in Your Word that I should be an example for other believers. Saying I am young is not an excuse. I have accepted You as my Savior, and that should show in how I talk and act. When others look at me, they should see that Jesus lives in my heart. They won't know that unless I love freely and choose to remain pure and faithful.

Father, I don't want to get off the path and find myself mixed up in the emptiness of this world. I want to start now, while I am young, a commitment to follow You and to stand out as a Christian. Give me strength to face the temptation to sample all the other options. I know the only true joy in this life comes from my walk with You. Use me to do great things, Father, even while I am young! Amen.

Commit your way to the LORD;
trust in him, and he will act.
PSALM 37:5 ESV

Day 196
Tell the Truth

Telling the truth should be an easy thing to do. I know it's right. I know Satan is the father of lies and that You are the Way, the Truth, and the Life. I want to do things Your way, Lord, but what about "little white lies"? Or maybe not telling all of the truth so I don't hurt someone's feelings? Does that count as lying?

I don't want to be left in the dark about things. I would much rather someone come to me and tell me what is going on, even if it is painful, so I think that is the best way for me to behave too. I think You honor truth, Lord. There's a verse in the Bible that talks about "speaking the truth in love" (Ephesians 4:15 NKJV). I think that means that we can be truthful, but at the same time we can be kind to others. It means speaking *truth*, not repeating gossip or our own and others' opinions. I think it means to speak Your truth found in Your Word.

God, help me to lovingly speak truth to others. Amen.

Gentle words are a tree of life;
a deceitful tongue crushes the spirit.
PROVERBS 15:4 NLT

No Pressure

Peer pressure. Temptations. Both of these bombard me nearly every day. I want to fit in, so sometimes I give in to peer pressure. Other times I'm tempted to say or act in an ungodly manner. I don't want to, but I do.

Father, the Bible says that sin came into this world when Adam and Eve disobeyed You. The devil tempted and deceived Eve, then she influenced Adam to disobey You too. After that, Adam blamed Eve! When what really happened is he caved in to temptation.

It's not so different today. Help me to avoid peer pressure and temptations so that I stay obedient to Your will for my life. If a friend pressures me to do something I shouldn't, please give me the courage and will to say no. When I'm tempted to do something wrong, give me the strength to stay on track.

Adam and Eve messed up, and sometimes I do too. But I'm grateful for Your forgiveness and the opportunity for another chance. Please help me to obey You and not accuse someone else for my failings. Amen.

The man replied, "It was the woman you gave me who gave me the fruit, and I ate it." Then the LORD God asked the woman, "What have you done?" "The serpent deceived me," she replied. "That's why I ate it."
GENESIS 3:12–13 NLT

Day 198
A Gift of Peace

Jesus, You tell me not to be troubled or afraid. . .and to accept Your gift of peace. . .and I want to do that more than anything. I don't know why I still let some problems get me down. I don't understand why I let myself get so scared and nervous about so many things! It shows my lack of faith, and I'm really sorry for that. Please help me to grow in my faith and trust in You.

I don't want to be scared of things. I want to live in peace and have confidence to do what You created me to do. I'm thankful for all the gifts You've given me, and I pray that You will give me courage to share them with others without fear.

Thank You for Your amazing gifts. I know that no one else can fill me with peace in my mind and heart like You do. Let me accept those gifts and remember them at all times. Amen.

"I am leaving you with a gift—peace of mind and heart. And the peace I give is a gift the world cannot give. So don't be troubled or afraid."
JOHN 14:27 NLT

Day 199
Loving Others

Lord Jesus, I know You tell me to love everyone. That's easy to do when they're nice to me or don't say or do something to hurt my feelings. But how can I do that when I don't even *like* some people? They say mean things about the way I look, gossip about me, and even laugh at me.

I read about people in the Bible who seem to me like it would be difficult to love. There were people who cheated others and those who had anger-management issues. Others disobeyed You, and Your own disciple even took a bribe to turn You over to those who would kill You. But You still loved them all.

Father, help me to remember that I'm not always so loveable either, but I'm still loved. There is never anything I can do to cause You to stop loving me. And I have friends and family who love me, even though we go through rough patches.

Please give me a heart to love others like You do—not based on whether I think they deserve it or not, but rather just because they are creations You have made and love, just like me. Amen.

"My command is this:
Love each other as I have loved you."
JOHN 15:12 NIV

Day 200
The Rumor Mill

Oops! Sometimes I get caught up in gossip, Lord. I don't mean to! Someone starts a rumor about someone else, and they tell me. Then I whisper the secret to a friend. I make her promise not to tell, but she breaks the promise and spreads the rumor to someone else. Before long, everyone knows. Problem is, sometimes the gossip isn't even true. Another problem. . .what we're saying hurts people's feelings sometimes, and I end up feeling really bad in the end.

Gossip is like a forest fire! It spreads and spreads and hurts a lot of people in the process. Can You help me put out the forest fire instead of spreading it, Father? When someone tells me some "juicy gossip," please close my mouth! Don't let me spread it to anyone else. Instead, remind me to pray for the person who's being gossiped about and to keep my heart pure. I want to be known as someone who brings people together, not someone who divides friends by gossiping. Amen.

Whoever covers an offense seeks love, but he who repeats a matter separates close friends.
PROVERBS 17:9 ESV

Harmful Humor

Lord, recently I was with some of my friends when they began teasing someone—someone who is not as fortunate as my friends and me. At first I thought the teasing was funny. Then I found myself almost joining in. But something inside of me—it must've been Your Spirit—told me that teasing this person was wrong. Instead of joining in, I began feeling embarrassed for my friends and sorry for the person they were mocking. Yet I did not have the courage to tell them to stop. So I just walked away.

Suddenly I realized that what some people consider humor can harm others. Since then I've tried to be more aware of what I am saying. After all, God, You made each one of us in Your image. That means that if we mock someone, we are also mocking You.

Help me, Lord, to be more mindful of my words, to find the courage to help others who are being teased, and to speak up when my friends are being unkind. Remind me that each one of us is special in Your eyes and worthy of praise. Amen.

Whoever mocks poor people insults their Creator;
gloating over misfortune is a punishable crime.
PROVERBS 17:5 MSG

Day 202
Love and Respect

I hear all the time about how loving and kind You are, God. I hear about Your compassion and mercy. It's comforting to know I can trust You and that You aren't out to get me.

But I've also heard that I should fear You. I want to understand better what that means. Why should I fear You if You're good and kind?

I guess it's kind of like having a healthy fear of my parents. I know they love me more than anything. But I also know that if I do something stupid, I'm going to pay for it. They punish me because they love me, and they want me to learn the best way to live.

I love You, Lord. I also understand that You are God, and if I go against Your ways, You will discipline me. The reason You discipline me is because You love me and You want the best for me. Thank You for loving me that much. Help me to always have the right kind of respect for Your ways, Lord. Amen.

"These are the ones I look on with favor: those who are humble and contrite in spirit, and who tremble at my word."
ISAIAH 66:2 NIV

Day 203
Depending on God

So often I just jump into things without talking it over with You, Lord. I want to do better about that. I want us to become so close that I wouldn't think of making plans without You. Can we be a team? Will You lead me and walk alongside me? I need Your help. Your Word assures me that if I rely on You in everything I set out to do, I will be successful. Because of Your great love for me, God, I want all my goals to be Jesus-centered. I want everything I seek to accomplish in this life to reflect my love for You. Be at the center of my thinking and guide me as I create goals for myself. As I get older, I will have even more decisions to make, such as where to go to school or what career to pursue. I will have choices regarding marriage and children, where to live, and all sorts of things. While I am young, I want to get into the habit of walking with You. I commit my ways to You, Lord. Please bless me and allow my plans to succeed. I will give You all the glory. Amen.

♥

Depend on the LORD in whatever you do,
and your plans will succeed.
PROVERBS 16:3 NCV

Blessed All Over Again

There are times when I grumble, whine, and complain about all the things I want but don't have. Instead of looking at how You have blessed my life, I find myself focusing on all that I lack.

Open my eyes, Lord, to everything around me. Help me to realize that in a world where so many people have so little, I have so very much.

Your Word tells me that it is so much more wonderful to give than to receive. Create in me a grateful spirit and a heart that cares to share. Show me what I might give away to bless the lives of others—whether it be a dress, a necklace, a grocery bag filled with food, or perhaps something as simple as a smile.

I know that when I give of myself—whether it is a material thing or an act of service—all thoughts of lack disappear. I am overcome with love and joy because I'm following Your law to love You and to love others as I love myself. When I make it all about pleasing You—by giving from the bottom of my heart and closet—I find myself blessed all over again! Amen.

All must give as they are able, according to the blessings given to them by the Lord your God.
DEUTERONOMY 16:17 NLT

Trust in the Lord

God, there have been times when I have trusted someone and he or she has really let me down. It hurts! After a while, it causes me not to trust anyone or anything. I find myself building walls between myself and others, only letting them in so far but not fully confiding in them or sharing my deepest feelings. I don't want to be rejected again or disappointed when someone doesn't remain true.

Help me to realize, Father, that it will always be a tricky balance to determine which people in my life to trust. But I can always trust You. You will never leave me or lead me down a wrong path. If I trust in You, You promise to direct me and to make Your plans clear to me as I journey through life. What an awesome promise!

And Lord, while we are talking about trust, please help me to take down the walls that I have constructed between myself and others. Give me wisdom about which friends I can trust, but help me to have an open heart and mind. I know that I need Christian friends in whom I can confide. Amen.

Those who know the LORD trust him, because he
will not leave those who come to him.
PSALM 9:10 NCV

God Understands

Lord, I am so frustrated. No one understands me. I guess they try, but my parents are so out of touch with what I am feeling. My friends are too concerned with their own problems to care about mine. I try to believe that You understand me. I know You created me and that You love me. But do You get it? Do You really get how hard this life can be?

I guess You do. You came down here from heaven. It must have been perfect there. The Bible says there are no tears and no pain in heaven. Why would You leave that glorious place to come to earth? It's because You wanted to be one of us, isn't it? You wanted people like me, years later, to know that You walked where we walked. You wanted me to know that I was worth it all—even leaving heaven, even giving Your life.

Jesus, when no one else understands me, remind me that You do. Even though You are God, You lived here as a child and grew into a man. You experienced this life. You get it. Thanks, Jesus. Amen.

He had to be one of us, so that he could serve God as our merciful and faithful high priest and sacrifice himself for the forgiveness of our sins.
HEBREWS 2:17 CEV

Curb My Words

Sometimes I blurt things out without thinking. I make a promise then I either forget it or I don't follow through. Other times, I retaliate and say things I shouldn't to my parents, family members, or friends. In a rush of emotions, I make comments that are often unkind or disrespectful.

That's not how I want to be, Lord. When You walked this earth, You watched Your words. You never reacted; You acted. Help me to choose my words wisely, to think before I speak, to consider before I make a promise.

I like to talk a lot, and that gets me into trouble sometimes. So please help me curb my words and direct my thoughts to think before I make comments that I can't take back. I want to become more like You. God, thank You for loving me even when my tongue gets ahead of my thinking! Amen.

Do not be too hasty to speak your mind before God or too quick to make promises you won't keep, for God is in heaven and you are on earth. Therefore, watch your tongue; let your words be few.
ECCLESIASTES 5:2 VOICE

Beauty from Inside

Creator God, show me what You see in me. Tell me how special I am to You. I was made in Your image, but sometimes I feel like I need to find acceptance in the way other people see me. I wish I didn't care about that so much. I'm sorry, Lord. Help me to base my self-image on the way You see me.

The commercials I see and all the advertising at the mall make me feel worthless sometimes! I don't look anything like that! Then I think about the most beautiful person I know, and she is beautiful because her heart is pure and she follows after You, not because she looks like a supermodel!

Your Word tells me that outward beauty doesn't last. Everyone gets old. And true beauty comes from inside the heart. So help me to follow You with a servant's heart and to bless You no matter what! Help me to live my life for You, and make me beautiful from the inside out. I know I'm worth a great deal to You. You gave Your life for me, after all! Amen.

Charm is deceptive, and beauty does not last; but a woman who fears the Lord will be greatly praised.
PROVERBS 31:30 NLT

Second Place

I'm so tired of feeling second best, Lord. Sometimes I feel like my parents like my brother or sister better than me. My friends all seem to have their "besties," but I'm not considered anyone's best friend. I feel invisible to other people in authority at times. There are so many things I attempt, only to feel like I fall second place to someone else—someone more talented, someone funnier, someone more popular, someone better than I am.

Father, thank You for not having favorites. I can run to You and know that You always have time for me and love me unconditionally because all of Your children are number one to You. Help me to continue doing my best, knowing it's for You...and that You're the only one who really matters. I don't want to keep trying to do better and better, only to fail again. But in Your eyes, I'm not a failure!

On days when I get discouraged, I ask that You comfort me in the way that only a best friend can. Thank You, Lord. Amen.

> "Look at the birds of the air: they neither sow nor reap nor gather into barns, and yet your heavenly Father feeds them. Are you not of more value than they?"
> MATTHEW 6:26 ESV

Day 210
As Pure as Snow

Father, I know so many girls who try too hard to get attention from boys. Sometimes I think they go overboard in the way they dress and act. Lord, I know the Bible says You want us to be pure not just in our hearts but in our outward appearance—the way we dress ourselves. Keep me from falling into the trap of wanting to dress like my friends or talk like my friends if it's not pleasing to You. What matters most is that people know I'm Yours!

And God, please work on my heart to make sure it's pure. My thoughts and attitudes need to be holy and as white as snow. I want You to look at me and smile because You're so pleased with how pure my heart is. Remind me every day, Lord, that staying in Your Word is the very best way to keep my heart innocent and clean. May I always shine like the glistening white snow for You!

How can a young person stay on the path of purity?
By living according to your word.
PSALM 119:9 NIV

An Attitude of Gratitude

Heavenly Father, sometimes I find myself complaining about everything or just being ungrateful in general. Things in my life aren't perfect, and I shouldn't expect them to be, but I usually want everything to be perfect and easy. Whenever I'm feeling this way, help me to remember and be thankful for everything that I do have and for how You have taken care of me in the past. Thank You for my family, my friends, and for all the ways You have blessed me. Thank You for creating this beautiful world and giving me a place to live. Thank You for giving me the opportunity to get an education and learn about things, and thank You for creating me just the way I am. Most of all, thank You for dying for my sins and giving me eternal life and the ability to share Your love with those around me. Amen.

Let your roots grow down into him, and let your lives be built on him. Then your faith will grow strong in the truth you were taught, and you will overflow with thankfulness.
COLOSSIANS 2:7 NLT

Day 212
Speak Up!

Lord, I love You with all my heart. But sometimes it's hard to talk about You in front of my friends. They don't all feel the same about You, and if I talk about You too much, they might think I'm weird.

It's not that I'm ashamed of You, Lord. I just don't always know how to bring You into the conversation. I want my friends to know about You. I want them to know how cool and awesome and amazing You are. I want them to know how much You love them.

But the words get jumbled and don't sound right. I don't want to come across as some kind of religious freak. I don't want to come across like I think I'm better or holier than the people around me.

Help me know how to tell others about You, Lord. Guide my words, my body language, my tone of voice. Help me know when to speak and when to stay quiet, showing Your love through my actions. Give me courage to talk about You and wisdom with the words I say. I want my words to point people to You. Amen.

♥

"I tell you," he replied,
"if they keep quiet, the stones will cry out."
LUKE 19:40 NIV

Honor Is Required

Lord, thank You for my mom and dad. You knew who my parents would be long before I was even born. You had a plan for me and a place for me. Thank You that my parents gave me life and a chance to grow up. I don't understand all the things they do, but You've said that I am to honor them, give them respect out of love for You.

So today, Lord, I want to honor them by being obedient and respectful. I may not agree with their decisions, and I may not like the way they interact with me, but help me not to be sassy or bratty, even behind their backs.

Lord, You are the One who created families. You knew that kids couldn't make it on their own, and so You gave them parents to help them out. You are my heavenly Father, and I'm so glad to belong to Your family too.

I ask You today to bless my mom and dad, even if they don't know You, and help me to honor them so we will all be closer to one another and to You. Amen.

*"Honor your father and your mother,
as the Lord your God has commanded you."*
Deuteronomy 5:16 nkjv

Slow to Speak

I seem to lose my temper more and more often, Lord. What's gotten into me? Perhaps it's because my body is changing so fast: one day I feel like a little girl, but the next day like a young woman. That can be so confusing— and frustrating. Then, feeling out of sorts, I find myself in a bad mood. Before I know it, I'm blurting out of my mouth whatever is in my head. But that's not what I want to do—or how I want to be!

Lord, words are powerful—they can wound so easily. So when things don't go the way I want them to, help me to calm myself down by taking a few deep breaths and whispering Your name. Help me to come from a place of peace before I open my mouth.

Give me the wisdom, Lord, to choose my words with care—or perhaps to just remain silent until I've thought things out a little more. Remind me that You would have me be quick to listen. Then—and only then—to speak. Amen.

Remember this, my dear friends! Everyone must be quick to listen, but slow to speak and slow to become angry. Human anger does not achieve God's righteous purpose.
JAMES 1:19–20 GNT

How Did I End Up Here?

Everyone else's families seem cooler than mine, God. I look at them and wonder how I ended up here. And yet, when we are all together, sometimes I couldn't imagine belonging to any other crazy group of people!

Thank You for giving me the family that You knew I needed. You have placed me in this particular family for a reason. Help me to look for ways to serve and honor my family. Remind me that while they meet many of my needs, I can also meet some of theirs—even while I am still young.

When I begin to question why I don't have a different type of family, teach me to trust in Your sovereignty. You don't make mistakes! I truly want to honor You in the way that I treat each member of my family. Even if they do not always treat me with respect, allow me to find it in my heart to show love, generosity, and genuine care. I love You, heavenly Father, and while no family is perfect, I thank You for choosing this one for me. It would be awfully lonely to live without a family. Amen.

God sets the lonely in families.
PSALM 68:6 NIV

Day 216
Be Still

I have too many things going on, Lord. I like everything I do, but sometimes it's just too much. From school every day to church activities to sports and dance and clubs, I don't even have time to change clothes, much less spend time with my friends.

Lord, I don't want to miss out on anything. I don't want to quit the things that are important to me. At the same time, I need a break. I need a rest. It feels like I never have time to just relax.

You told us to be still, Lord. That sounds good, but to be honest, I don't know if I can. Every time I get still and quiet for even five minutes, I feel like I'm going crazy. I want to take a break, but my mind just keeps going and going, even when my body gets still.

Help me to be still and just listen to You, Lord. Thank You for holding me close and for teaching me what it means to be calm and to just relax in You. Help me focus my thoughts on You and just relax in Your love today. Amen.

"Be still, and know that I am God."
PSALM 46:10 NIV

Gossip—Not Cool!

We all have secrets. I know I do, and so do my friends. But I am careful with whom I share my secrets because some girls gossip; although I confess that I have gossiped too.

Father, I don't want to gossip, so please help me to avoid others who spread rumors about everyone and everything! They're not my friends. Instead, I desire to become a good example. If a friend confides in me, help me to keep her words in confidence. I ask to become more trustworthy every day with Your help.

It seems that girls especially love to gossip. Although I'm not sure why, it's the way it is. But as a child of Yours, I know that You expect more from me. My desire is to obey You, not my foolish thoughts and ramblings. It's not cool to bad-mouth someone else behind her back. Give me the courage to silence the gossiper and my own temptations to gossip. Amen.

A gossip goes around telling secrets, but those who are trustworthy can keep a confidence.
PROVERBS 11:13 NLT

Heaven's Reward

I've been so busy, Lord. Probably too busy. Help me to slow down and keep my priorities straight. School and grades and friends and college are all good things to strive for, but I know this is all just a journey that will lead me to eternity with You. Help me to keep my heart set on that as I accomplish goals here on earth.

Help me to do my best work, Lord. I want all this to be for Your glory, not mine. I hope people will see You at work in me as I grow older and set out on the path You have planned for me. Knowing and living by that truth gives me confidence to use my gifts and talents to complete whatever work comes my way.

Thank You that You have set eternity right here in my heart (Ecclesiastes 3:11). Allow me to keep heaven in my mind during each task and milestone. Amen.

Work willingly at whatever you do, as though you were working for the Lord rather than for people. Remember that the Lord will give you an inheritance as your reward, and that the Master you are serving is Christ.
COLOSSIANS 3:23–24 NLT

Day 219
Wait!

Sometimes things take such a long time, Father. I have to wait in a line when I have other places I need to go. I lose my cell signal, so I can't call my friend back. And I have to wait *forever* for the bathroom to get ready for school.

Some days it feels like everything is moving so slowly. I have tons of things to do, and it never seems like there's enough time.

I guess I should be patient, Lord, but that's so much easier to say than do. Maybe I'm moving too fast. And I suppose I'm being a little bit selfish too, because I'm sure other people want to have their turn.

Please help me to learn to slow down, Jesus. Let me take a breath and learn how to wait. A lot of good things take time: flowers growing, good friendships, even a cake baking. None of that can be hurried. Help me to be patient like You want me to be. Amen.

See how the farmer waits for the precious fruit of the earth, being patient about it, until it receives the early and the late rains. You also, be patient.
JAMES 5:7–8 ESV

Day 220
Getting My Way

Oh boy, am I stubborn sometimes, Lord! I want to stomp my foot when I don't get my own way, to demand that people give me what I want. And if they don't give it to me, sometimes my attitude really stinks. Oh, help! I need You to remind me every day that what really matters isn't getting my own way; it's humbling myself in Your presence and becoming more like You. Can You help me with this...pretty please?

Jesus didn't demand His own way. He prayed and asked His Father (You!) what to do...then He did it. No arguments. No foot stomping. He listened and then obeyed. I want to be like Jesus, Father! That means I have to get rid of my pride. No more demanding. No more foot stomping. From now on, Lord, I will watch my attitude and humble myself. Amen.

Pride goes before destruction,
a haughty spirit before a fall.
PROVERBS 16:18 NIV

Day 221
Envy

God, I struggle with envy a lot. Whenever my friends get the latest phone or new clothes, I want the same things, and it makes me miserable. And whenever I am jealous of my friends, it makes me act unkindly toward them, and I know that isn't right. Please help me to be happy for them when good things come their way. I would want them to be happy for me if our roles were reversed, and I don't want to be jealous—it's an ugly attitude. Help me to be content with the things that I do have and to be thankful for having so much when so many people in the world have so little. Thank You for giving me parents who provide for me and take care of my needs. I know that true happiness and joy don't come from what I have; they come from walking with You and looking at everything in my life with gratitude. So next time one of my friends gets new clothes or a new phone, remind me to be happy for her and not compare what she has to what I have. Amen.

I realized the reason people work hard and try to succeed: They are jealous of each other. This, too, is useless, like chasing the wind.

ECCLESIASTES 4:4 NCV

Day 222
Surprises and Wonders

Lord, many of my friends seem to be playing follow the leader. Everyone does what everyone else is doing—whether it's wrong or right. But *You* are the true leader. You are the hero that will never fall. So I want to follow and imitate You—not the latest movie star, American idol, sports figure, or even the most popular kid in school.

Each and every day, Lord, renew my mind. Keep me from blindly following the latest fad or idol. Instead of worshipping the things and people of this world, I want to worship You—and You alone. With my eyes on You, I know I will be following Your direction for my life. Open my ears to Your words, and give me courage to walk the path You have laid out for me, for I know it holds amazing surprises and wonders I can only imagine.

If I take a course that seems different to others, I'm okay with that, for I know You will always be with me no matter what I do or where I go. Thank You for leading me *Your* way. Amen.

Do not conform to the pattern of this world, but be transformed by the renewing of your mind. Then you will be able to test and approve what God's will is.
ROMANS 12:2 NIV

Day 223
What about Me?

Heavenly Father, sometimes I feel weary from all this "doing good" stuff. Things like volunteering at the local animal shelter, donating new and used items to charity (books, clothes, toys. . .), and numerous little acts of unremembered kindness that I do throughout the year have me all worn out! To be completely honest, God, I wonder if it's worth all the effort. I mean, does it really matter all that much. . .does anyone notice?

Your Word reminds us that we should keep on doing good. You promise to reward us for all our effort (Galatians 6:9). Because of Your promise, Father, I'm asking that You help me to keep my focus on others instead of myself. I know You *always* see what I do to make a difference in the world, even when others don't see or don't care. And if You see, then that's enough for me! When others overlook or forget my kindness, it is so wonderful to know that You never will!

Please help me to keep up the good work, God. And I'll be looking to see what good things You have in store for me. Amen.

♥

Let us not become weary in doing good,
for at the proper time we will reap a
harvest if we do not give up.
GALATIANS 6:9 NIV

Day 224
Loving Others

It is so easy to love others when they treat me nicely, Lord. The tough part comes when they don't! Your Word commands me to love even my enemies; so, certainly I need to show love to my friends and family members at all times. But that is a tall order!

Help me, Father, to remember how much You love me. While I was yet a sinner, You sent Jesus to earth. You allowed Your only Son to die a terrible death on the cross that I might have life. You put Him on that cross in place of me. You loved me that much!

And so, when others leave me out or hurt my feelings, let me react with love. When I am in a bad mood, help me to control my tongue. Sometimes my careless words can really hurt those around me. I want to be a girl who is known for her love. I want to outdo everyone in showing love and respect, going beyond what is expected. I want to surprise others with my love. Give me this type of heart, I pray, Lord.

Love one another with brotherly affection.
Outdo one another in showing honor.
ROMANS 12:10 ESV

A True Friend

"It takes being a friend to have one." I've heard that quote before, Lord, and I truly believe it. Help me to be a good friend. When I consider what that means, I realize I often fall short. No one is perfect, but I desire to be a better friend. I want to be a good listener and someone who is trustworthy. Teach me to compromise with my friends, sometimes doing what they want to do rather than always seeking to have my own way. Make me the type of friend who respects others, not someone who is two-faced, acting one way in my friend's presence and then talking bad about her behind her back. I don't like it when someone does that to me. I never want to hurt someone in that manner.

God, You have blessed me with some good friends. Help me to be thankful for them and to treat them kindly even when we disagree. And where there is a need in my life for a friend, lead me to one who will be a true friend to me. I need wisdom as I choose godly friends. Amen.

Then Jonathan made a covenant with David
because he loved him as himself.
1 SAMUEL 18:3 NASB

Day 226
What's Important

It's hard not to want what money can buy. All the latest clothes, makeup, electronic gadgets—my list is endless. I know those things aren't important, so I need to focus on what is more important than anything I might own. What takes priority in my life are relationships—namely, my relationship with You, God.

Even though I can't see You, God, I know that You are there. I know You are good and that You love me beyond what I can imagine. I want to know You better. The only way to do that is to read the Bible more. Your Word tells me who You are, and the truth found there helps me understand what You have to say about Yourself. I know there are a lot of opinions about who You are, and there are many people who can help me learn, but I need to go to the Source—You.

There is so much I don't know and can't understand about You, God! But thank You for giving us the Bible to read. Give me more understanding of who You are. Amen.

"Yes, a person is a fool to store up earthly wealth
but not have a rich relationship with God."
Luke 12:21 NLT

What about Popularity?

Popularity. It's something every girl my age thinks about. To me, popularity means other kids like to be around me or think I'm pretty. People, especially boys, gravitate toward the girls who are popular.

Yet, when I read the Word of God, it never encourages that kind of popularity. Instead, You are pleased with a teachable, loving, compassionate, understanding, and Christ-centered heart and life.

Titus and another worker were popular for preaching the gospel. They were trustworthy and honorable men who loved You and cared little about pleasing others to gain approval.

When I seek popularity, Father, I want the kind that Your followers had. I want other kids to look at me and see You, not what I'm wearing or how pretty I am. Outer beauty doesn't last, but inner beauty remains forever. That's the kind of popularity I desire, Lord. Amen.

I thank God for giving Titus the same devoted concern for you that I have. He was most considerate of how we felt. . . . We're sending a companion along with him, someone very popular in the churches for his preaching of the Message. But there's far more to him than popularity. He's rock-solid trustworthy. The churches handpicked him to go with us as we travel about doing this work of sharing God's gifts.
2 Corinthians 8:16–19 MSG

Day 228
God Is Love

Loving You, Lord, shows the rest of the world that I am Yours and You are mine. I am so glad and amazed and thankful that You sent Your Son for me to die in my place and take all the sin and shame for all of my past, present, and future mistakes. You've already paid for them all! I just can't wrap my brain around that, Lord. But I'm so very thankful.

And by asking You to make Your home inside my heart, You gave me Your Spirit to lead me and guide me on my way to eternity with You. What a miracle! Thank You! Please give me ears to hear when Your Spirit is leading me in my heart. I want to listen to Your still, small voice that gives me wisdom and truth.

Help me to love people, Lord. Even the difficult ones. And help me to love You with all of my heart and my soul and my strength. Amen.

Whoever does not love does not know God,
because God is love. This is how God showed
his love among us: He sent his one and only Son
into the world that we might live through him.
1 JOHN 4:8–9 NIV

Everyday Blessings

Father, thank You for the many good things You give to me and do for me! I just love sleepovers with friends and laughing with them until my face—or my stomach—hurts. I love all the shades of a beautiful sunset. I love it when I have a few free moments and I can actually decide how *I* want to spend them.

I love texting with my friends. I love a new pair of shoes. . .especially if there was a really good sale!

I love a warm drink on a cold day. I love birthday parties and spending time with those who are important to me.

I love a good movie, my favorite song, giving my friend that "perfect gift," finding something that had been lost that I thought I'd never see again, and answers to prayer.

All of these good things come from You, Lord Jesus. I have done nothing to deserve them, but You have given them to me anyway. You are so good! Thank You! Amen.

How great is your goodness that you have stored up for those who fear you, that you have given to those who trust you. You do this for all to see.
PSALM 31:19 NCV

Day 230
What Joy!

Okay, I'll be honest, Lord. . .I don't always have a happy heart. Sometimes I have icky days and just want to scream or cry. But You tell me to praise my way through the hard times, to lift my voice and give You praise, even when things are going bad. Sounds hard, but I'm going to give it a try! I know people in the Bible did it and it worked for them, so that must mean it will work for me too!

I want my heart to be filled with joy. When people look at me, I want them to say, "Wow! That girl is always smiling! She seems so full of joy and life!" I don't want a fake smile. I want a real one!

I know that real joy comes from spending time with You, Father. Remind me of that when I start to feel down, okay? Don't let me slip too far away from You. Keep my heart close to Yours so that Your joy will fill me up, bubbling inside of me until it spills over onto everything I see each day. What fun that will be, to live a joyous life! Amen.

Above all else, guard your heart,
for everything you do flows from it.
PROVERBS 4:23 NIV

Day 231
My Temple

Dear God, I want to take better care of my body, not just to look pretty but to be healthy and honor the body that You have created and given me. So whenever I am tempted to eat more than I'm hungry for or just sit on the couch all day, I need to remember that probably isn't the best thing for my body. And it's so hard for me to get all the rest I need sometimes—I'd rather stay up and hang out with my friends or read late into the night than give my body what it really needs: sleep. So please help me to have self-control when it comes to taking care of my body and making sure that I am treating it with the respect it deserves. I want to glorify You with every action I make; continue to teach me how to do that. Amen.

You surely know that your body is a temple where the Holy Spirit lives. The Spirit is in you and is a gift from God. You are no longer your own. God paid a great price for you. So use your body to honor God.
1 CORINTHIANS 6:19–20 CEV

Being Beautiful

Dear God, I want to be beautiful. I don't think any girl wants *not* to be beautiful. There are diets to try, clothes to buy, and cosmetic products to use. There are exercises to make you fit and hairstyles to make you glamorous.

You made us with the desire for beauty; You created us to bring beauty to Your world. But You also made us to be Yours first; our beauty is to reflect Your glory.

I need You to help me make good decisions in what I do to my body. Help me remember to pray about how I dress and walk and act. Help me remember to ask for Your guidance when I'm in the clothing store, and let me look in the mirror every morning and think about the message I'm sending to others as they see the way I'm dressed for the day.

God, I know that beauty in the soul is the thing that will last forever; develop in me a beautiful spirit and help me to honor You with my face and body all the days of my life. Amen.

You should clothe yourselves instead with the beauty that comes from within, the unfading beauty of a gentle and quiet spirit, which is so precious to God.
1 PETER 3:4 NLT

Day 233
Future Friends

Sometimes I fight with them and sometimes I stick up for them, but Lord, my siblings are here to stay. We're part of the same family, yet we're very different. They really bug me a lot of the time. My mom says that someday we'll be good friends and I hope so, but it's hard to imagine that right now.

I've heard about siblings in the Bible, and some of the stories aren't very good: Cain killed his brother Abel; Rachel was jealous of her sister, Leah; and Jacob swindled his brother out of his inheritance. I don't want to be known as that kind of sibling!

Maybe one of the reasons You put me into a family is so I would learn to share and think about somebody besides me. Even though I don't get along with them all the time, I do love my siblings, and I want us to have a good relationship someday.

Help me remember to think before I speak and to respect their space and their stuff. Show me how to be kind even when I don't feel like it. Amen.

A friend is always loyal, and a brother
is born to help in time of need.
PROVERBS 17:17 NLT

Day 234
Like an Eagle

Lord, every once in a while when I'm trying to do something—get good grades, do well in sports, or serve You—I get frustrated, tired, and want to give up. I lose faith and confidence in myself, thinking I can't do anything right. That I've let down my parents, teachers, and friends. But then I remember as long as I look to and hope in You, I will get strong again—and perhaps get the grade, make the team, or find an awesome way to lend a helping hand to others.

Give me the strength to keep trying and trying. If I stumble and fall, pick me up off the ground. Don't let me get down on myself, but help me rise up to the next challenge that comes my way. Give me the energy to soar like an eagle, going above the clouds, and rising up to meet Your love and power. The more I practice flying, the stronger my wings will become and the better I will be able to serve You. Amen.

Even youths grow tired and weary, and. . . stumble and fall; but those who hope in the LORD will renew their strength. They will soar on wings like eagles; they will run and not grow weary, they will walk and not be faint.
ISAIAH 40:30–31 NIV

Day 235
Decisions Big and Small

Decisions, decisions. Some are easy—like what to eat for breakfast, wear to school, or choose for dessert. Then there are the harder decisions—like what I want to be when I'm more grown up, what I should study for that next test, or what after-school activities to sign up for. Sometimes it takes me so long to figure out what I want to do—or what I *should* do—that I miss out on awesome opportunities.

Next time I have a decision to make, Lord, remind me to spend some time asking You for Your thoughts. I know I don't have all the answers—but I am sure *You* do! And I know You will show me the right way to go—no matter if the decision is big or small. You are concerned with everything I am and do. So, I leave it all in Your hands and wait to hear Your voice saying, "Here is the road. Follow it" (Isaiah 30:21 GNT). Amen.

Guide me by your truth and instruct me.
You keep me safe, and I always trust you.
PSALM 25:5 CEV

Day 236
No Fear

The unknown is scary. So much is going on in this world, God. When I think about what could happen, I sometimes feel afraid. What if someone tries to harm me or my family? What if I lose someone close to me? What if something bad happens?

The weight of all this presses down on me. I don't know how to stop thinking about it. I know that King David, though he was a mighty warrior, was sometimes afraid too. In Psalm 56:3 (NLT) he says, "But when I am afraid, I will put my trust in you."

Can it be that simple? To trust—to depend on You—to keep me and my family safe? But I know bad things can happen, even to those who love You, Lord. I don't have control of the circumstances in my life, but I can choose how I will respond to them.

David decided not to let fear control him. Don't let it control me either, God. Help me to trust in You when I am afraid. Amen.

You can go to bed without fear; you will lie down and sleep soundly. You need not be afraid of sudden disaster or the destruction that comes upon the wicked, for the LORD is your security. He will keep your foot from being caught in a trap.
PROVERBS 3:24–26 NLT

I Will Complete This!

Chores—I dislike them! Homework—ugh! Responsibilities like these annoy me sometimes. Yet I know they're a big part of my life and growth.

Lord, sometimes I'm into my work, eager and ready to do well. I start a school project, enthused and excited, only to feel differently when the project becomes difficult. Or I start to clean or decorate my room only to give up halfway. I want to finish; I desire to do well in anything and everything I try. But my weaknesses and laziness get in the way.

The scriptures tell me to finish what I start; to keep going when I want to give up; to complete any task to the best of my abilities. Help me, Father, when I'm tempted to quit, especially when I'm doing things I don't particularly like to do in the first place—like unloading the dishwasher! Amen.

♥

The best thing you can do right now is to finish what you started. . .and not let those good intentions grow stale. Your heart's been in the right place all along. You've got what it takes to finish it up, so go to it.
2 CORINTHIANS 8:10–11 MSG

Day 238
Food and Clothes

God, it seems many of the girls around me obsess over food and clothes. I get caught up in it too—comparing myself to other girls who are skinnier and so I worry about food and eating too much and wondering if I look fat.

And clothes! I'm always checking the mirror and wishing I had new things or trying on outfits and hoping my friends don't realize I wore the same thing recently.

It's kinda funny that this verse is speaking directly to me today, when You said it first thousands of years ago! But I have a feeling You even had me in mind when You said it to Your followers a long time ago. Thanks for the reality check, Jesus. My life and my body were created by You to carry out Your plans for my life. Worrying about clothes and food is not pleasing to You.

Help me to have a good balance. Enjoying shopping and eating healthy foods is a good thing! But obsessing over it isn't. Help me not to worry about little stuff that doesn't really matter. Amen.

Jesus said, "That is why I tell you not to worry about everyday life—whether you have enough food to eat or enough clothes to wear. For life is more than food, and your body more than clothing."
LUKE 12:22–23 NLT

The Rough Places

Lord, I know You never promised life would be fair. As a matter of fact, it seems like the more hard stuff we go through, the more we have to depend on You to help us deal with it. And I guess that makes us better people.

Come to think of it, some of the nicest, gentlest, kindest people I know are people who have been through some really hard things. Maybe their parents are divorced, or they've had someone close to them die, or they've lived through some other real hardship.

I always want to pray for things to go smoothly in my life, Lord. But I wonder if it's not the rough places that help smooth out my character. I'm not going to ask You to make my life hard, Lord. That would be crazy. But I will pray that You use the difficult things in my life to make me more like You. Make me kinder, gentler, and more loving so I can make a positive difference in this world. Amen.

Count it all joy, my brothers, when you meet trials of various kinds, for you know that the testing of your faith produces steadfastness. And let steadfastness have its full effect, that you may be perfect and complete, lacking in nothing.

JAMES 1:2–4 ESV

Day 240
Lovely Petals

Lord, sometimes I think my relationship with You is like a flower opening up on a sunny day. That sweet little flower starts as a teeny-tiny seed that's planted deep in the ground, protected by the soil around it. After a little time goes by, little green sprouts grow up out of the soil. Before long, a little tightly closed bud appears on the vine. It drinks in the sun and water, preparing itself for what's about to come. Then, finally, the bud opens up for everyone to see—a gorgeous flower!

I'm like that little flower, Father! When I gave You my heart, You planted my little seed of faith, and now it's growing, growing, growing! Every day another petal opens up as I change and grow to become more like You. I pray that my relationship with You will be as sweet and as lovely as a rose in full bloom. When my friends and family spend time with me, I hope they see just how much I'm becoming like You. Amen.

And we know that in all things God works for the good of those who love him, who have been called according to his purpose.
ROMANS 8:28 NIV

Day 241
When I Need Courage

Dear Lord, I get scared of things so easily. Sometimes I still think there is a monster under my bed, and I don't want to put my feet down in the dark! And then there are real fears, like when I go to a new school and I don't know anyone and I'm scared to talk. When I'm in a new situation like that, give me courage to reach out and talk to people. Or if someone is new at my school, give me the courage to say hi and try to make them feel welcome. You can give me courage in every situation; I just need to call on You, and You are there. Thank You for Your promise to give me courage when I need it and for reminding me that You are there when I forget. So whenever I'm afraid, give me the courage that I need and the ability to use that courage for Your glory. Amen.

But Jesus immediately said to them:
"Take courage! It is I. Don't be afraid."
MATTHEW 14:27 NIV

Never Disappointed

Sometimes my life feels like one big disappointment after another, Lord. My grades aren't what I hoped they'd be. A friend promises to call or text and doesn't. I don't get chosen for the team, or when I do get chosen, I strike out.

I hate feeling disappointed all the time, Lord. I want to feel happy and excited about life, but it's hard when things don't go my way. How am I supposed to have a positive outlook when life keeps letting me down?

You said to put my hope in You. You promised to never leave me. No matter what happens in life, Your love never changes. Your goodness never fails. Your kindness continues forever.

I guess if I stop counting on things I can't control for my happiness and start counting on You alone, my attitude might change. I know that no matter how life disappoints me, You will always be there pouring beautiful things into my spirit. Your goodness doesn't change like my circumstances. If I put my hope in You, I'll never be disappointed. Amen.

"Then you will know that I am the LORD;
those who hope in me will not be disappointed."
ISAIAH 49:23 NIV

Day 243
Ordinary Days

O God, today I feel depressed, and I'm not sure why. There isn't really anything big wrong with my life, but I am bored and I feel stuck in the same pattern. My routine feels monotonous; I want something different and exciting to happen. Maybe that's the danger in watching television and movies; the lives of the stars seem much more interesting than mine.

I don't like ordinary days, but I remember that ordinary days were common in the Bible too. It wasn't every day that the Red Sea parted or lions' mouths were shut or giants were killed; most days were humble and ordinary. And I suppose that Moses wouldn't have been at the Red Sea if he hadn't put in all those ordinary days in the desert, and David wouldn't have killed Goliath if he hadn't spent ordinary days practicing with his sling.

I think I'd like to have exciting things happen all the time, but maybe that wouldn't be good for me. I need to learn to follow You in everyday stuff so that I'll be ready when the big stuff happens. Thank You for being there in all my very ordinary days. Amen.

Surely your goodness and unfailing love
will pursue me all the days of my life.
PSALM 23:6 NLT

Quietly Hoping

Sometimes I want answers *now*, Lord. I just don't want to wait. But when I am patient, really seek out Your Word and will, and look for Your help, hard times don't seem so hard.

People talk about "the patience of Job," a man who had everything until his family, crops, animals, and health were wiped out. But through it all, Job never turned away from You. Instead, he continued to have faith. And in the end, You blessed Job more than ever before!

It's all about trusting You. Once I can get that idea in my head, I'm ready to do some more waiting. To be patient, quietly hoping in You, certain that You'll work everything out someday, somehow. You will find a way to bless me as long as my heart is in the right place, my mind calm, my spirit hopeful, and my faith sure. Thank You, Lord, for what You are about to do today and tomorrow.

GOD proves to be good to the man who passionately waits, to the woman who diligently seeks. It's a good thing to quietly hope, quietly hope for help from GOD. It's a good thing when you're young to stick it out through the hard times.
LAMENTATIONS 3:25 MSG

Day 245
A True Daughter

It's hard for me to love people who have hurt me—especially if I didn't really like them to begin with. But, Jesus, You say we are to not only love those *close* to us but to love even our enemies! That seems like a really tough thing to ask. Yet I know that's just what You did to those who beat, mocked, and crucified You.

I know that if I pray for the power to love others—friends *and* enemies—I am sure to receive it. So help me today, Lord. Give me the strength to love all people. Give me the words to say when I meet those who have bullied me and the words to pray when I think of them. I want to be like You, Jesus. I want a heart as big as Yours.

God, give me the peace that goes beyond all understanding. Make me royalty—a true daughter of You, my King and Father in heaven. Mold me into a princess of peace with love and prayers for all. Amen.

"You have heard the law that says, 'Love your neighbor' and hate your enemy. But I say, love your enemies! Pray for those who persecute you! In that way, you will be acting as true children of your Father in heaven."
MATTHEW 5:43–45 NLT

You Know Me

God, You know me better than I know myself! You know when I stand up and when I sit down. You know what I'm thinking before I even say it (Psalm 139). The psalmist says that he can hardly comprehend what this means. I can't either.

Being known that well—being seen that clearly by You—might seem kind of risky. But You know me and love me anyway! That makes me feel very secure and safe. There is nothing hidden from You, God. Nothing about me surprises You. Yet You love me—no matter what I do, You still offer this incredible, unconditional love to me.

This only makes me want to love You back! But even with this I need Your help. I can't do it on my own. I don't know how. Like the psalmist, I'm asking for Your guidance and direction, for You to show me the way to love You more.

Give me eyes to see like You see me, God. Show me what I need to keep doing and what I need to change. Amen.

Search me, O God, and know my heart; test me and know my anxious thoughts. Point out anything in me that offends you, and lead me along the path of everlasting life.
PSALM 139:23–24 NLT

My Heavenly Father Knows Best

Sometimes I think I know what's best. I want to choose my own clothes, where I go to school, and make my own decisions.

Forgive me when I think that I know better than my parents—or You! When I try to figure out everything on my own, I usually get even more confused and frustrated. The truth is, I need my parents' advice and guidance, and I need Yours. I want to listen to them and to You, Lord. You have given me my parents to raise and look after me. So why do I object so much, especially when things don't go as I'd like?

I guess trusting You (and my parents) means allowing You to work in my life without my constant interference. I know that You and my parents are only trying to keep me on the right course. Remind me of that when I think I know what's best for me. Help me to follow and depend on You more and me less. Amen.

♥

Trust God from the bottom of your heart; don't try to figure out everything on your own. Listen for God's voice in everything you do, everywhere you go; he's the one who will keep you on track. Don't assume that you know it all.
PROVERBS 3:5–6 MSG

Day 248
Peace and Thankfulness

Father God, please give me a heart full of peace and thankfulness. What a difference I could make in my family and school if I always lived my life with a thankful heart! And if I let peace take control in my soul, not worrying about things that don't matter and trusting You no matter what happens? My friends and family would take notice! They would see Your real power shining through me!

When problems come that teach me lessons about growing in my faith...I can be thankful!

When life gets harder than I thought it would...I can have peace that You see what's going on and will be with me!

If something bad happens that I wasn't expecting and causes me to get closer to You...I can be thankful.

If my plans don't work out and I have to start something all over again...I can have peace that You know what's best for me.

I'm so glad You have my heart, Lord. We'll get through this life with peace and thankfulness...together! Amen.

♥

And let the peace that comes from Christ rule in your hearts. For as members of one body you are called to live in peace. And always be thankful.
COLOSSIANS 3:15 NLT

Day 249
Help!

Lord Jesus, I can get really stressed sometimes. I begin to worry, and then my heart begins to race, my palms get sweaty, and I feel like it's difficult to breathe.

The stress comes when I begin taking the test that I studied hours for, but then find that I must not have studied the right material.

The tension builds when I need to get up and talk or perform in front of people.

I get anxious when the other girls are talking about something that makes me feel uncomfortable.

Father, I don't want to be ruled by stress. I need to learn to turn to You in those moments and ask You for help. You have promised to hear me, to help me, and to give me peace. Please settle my mind and take my anxiety away. Thank You! In Jesus' name, amen.

Commit everything you do to the LORD.
Trust him, and he will help you.
PSALM 37:5 NLT

Day 250
Sassy!

Lord, sometimes my mouth gets me in trouble. Talk about smarting off! I can be the "Smarty-Pants Queen" sometimes! I don't mean to be sassy or cranky, but sometimes it happens. When it does, I wind up in trouble and also wind up feeling ashamed.

Please help me get rid of the attitude. It's like a trap! Once I start going down that road, I can't seem to turn back. In my heart I wish I could, but it's so hard! I know I look bad when I don't pay attention to how I speak to others, especially adults. Calm me down from the inside out. Put Your hand over my mouth so I don't say too much or speak in anger. I want to react calmly to people, not like a smarty-pants!

I see better days ahead, Father! You are controlling my heart and my mouth. You're calming my heart when I get worked up. You're reminding me every time I get "sassy" that it breaks Your heart. You're never sassy with me, after all! Amen.

Set a guard, O Lord, over my mouth;
keep watch over the door of my lips!
Psalm 141:3 esv

Day 251
I'm Not Strong Enough

Heavenly Father, sometimes I feel like I can't do something, like when I need to forgive a friend and I just don't think I can do it alone. When I feel this way, I need to talk to You and ask You to give me strength and the ability to forgive. I want to be able to do everything on my own and with my own strength, but I know I am not capable of that on my own. And when I feel this way, I know that You are there; You are my rock and my refuge. I can never forget that because of how many times You have demonstrated that in the past, and I know You will continue to demonstrate it in the future. Thank You for always giving me strength when I think that what I'm trying to accomplish is beyond me; I don't know what I would do without Your presence in my life and Your hand guiding me through all of the ups and downs. Thankfully I never have to worry about that! Amen.

It is God who arms me with
strength and keeps my way secure.
PSALM 18:32 NIV

Day 252
Sing a Song

Music is such an important part of my life, Lord. My friends and I listen to the latest songs. We know all the words to dozens of hits. We sing and dance to them, and watch reality shows on television, and vote to find the newest, next big-music sensation. We even try to do our hair and dress like the winners.

Singing along with the radio may be fun, but it's not the same as having a song in my heart. Having a song in my heart means I'm thinking about You and praising You all the time. Having a song in my heart means I'm happy with who You are and who I am in You. It means even when I'm thinking about other things, You're always there, in the back of my mind.

Lord, hit songs and popular singers will come and go, but You will always stay the same. During my lifetime, I'll probably know the words to hundreds of songs. I'll probably forget the words to hundreds more. But one thing will remain, and that's Your love for me. You will never leave me, never fail me, never forget me. And that's something worth singing about. Amen.

Sing and make music from
your heart to the Lord.
EPHESIANS 5:19 NIV

Choosing Friends

Thank You, Jesus, for my friends. They are there for me in the hard days and the fun days. I'm glad that I have friends to hang out with.

I know it is important for me to choose good friends. The Bible tells of people who chose the wrong kind of friends and how that affected them; I'm thinking of Baalam and how he was influenced to curse Israel and David who made an agreement with a pagan king. But then there are stories of people in the Bible whose friends were a blessing to them—Daniel and his three Hebrew friends who refused to bow down to idols, and Mary, Martha, and Lazarus who were earthly friends with Jesus and let Him share their home and food.

I want to have good friends, and I want to be a good friend. Give me wisdom so I can choose wisely; help me observe the things they like, the attitude they have, and what they post on Twitter and Facebook before I decide to hang with them. I want to be smart in choosing friends because if I stay friends with them, I will become like them. I'm asking for Your guidance. Amen.

Do not be misled: "Bad company
corrupts good character."
1 CORINTHIANS 15:33 NIV

True Success

Success can mean so many different things to so many different people. For me right now, success is making good grades, playing a game well, and getting to know You better. When I'm older, success might mean getting a good job, finding a nice husband, and serving at church on Sundays. But You, Lord, have a different meaning of success.

To You, true *success* means going all out for You! It means my reading or thinking about Your Word day and night, looking for Your direction, doing what You want me to do, and imitating Your Son, Jesus.

If I do that, I will not only be wise, making the right decisions, but will be seeing everything and everyone with Your eyes. In other words, I will see the good in all things. So Lord, I pray that You will help me to prosper in all I do, think, and say. Make Yourself clear to me when I read my Bible. Make me Your success story. Amen.

This Book of the Law shall not depart out of your mouth, but you shall meditate on it day and night, that you may observe and do according to all that is written in it. For then you shall make your way prosperous, and then you shall deal wisely and have good success.
JOSHUA 1:8 AMPC

God's Plans

What a declaration You have made upon my life, God! I make lists of things I'd like to do, places I'd like to go. But to know that the Almighty God of the universe has plans for me is pretty amazing. The Bible says You knit me together in my mother's womb. You know the number of hairs on my head. And You want only the very best for me. Help me, Lord, to discover Your will for my life and never reject it to go my own way. I know that You are at work already preparing me for the future.

As a jigsaw puzzle is put together one piece at a time, You will show me the next step to take at just the right time. I can imagine You gazing upon the whole puzzle, already intact. You can see the beautiful picture that one day will be revealed to me. For now, I will just live this day for You. I will walk and talk with You. I will read Your Word and follow Your commands. Thank You for the knowledge that You have plans full of hope and goodness for me! Amen.

"For I know the plans I have for you," says the LORD. "They are plans for good and not for disaster, to give you a future and a hope."
JEREMIAH 29:11 NLT

Day 256
Beauty

What do I do when I don't like what I see in the mirror? Some things about myself are impossible to change, God. How can I see myself as truly beautiful?

That only works when I look in Your mirror, not mine. When I see myself as You see me. You created me. You formed me. You love me just as I appear now. I don't need to change myself to be accepted or loved by You.

The world is so different from You, God! TV and magazines say that to be beautiful you have to be a certain size or wear the newest fashion. Even at school there seems to be a club of "beautiful people," and I don't fit in it. Is it possible they are wrong? You created me, so I must be beautiful!

Lord, I want to believe I'm beautiful, but *feeling* beautiful is a different story. The more I become like You, the more beautiful I will be. Make me beautiful on the inside, Lord. Amen.

Christ's love makes the church whole. His words evoke her beauty. Everything he does and says is designed to bring the best out of her, dressing her in dazzling white silk, radiant with holiness.
EPHESIANS 5:26–27 MSG

I Can Trust God

I often wonder whom I can trust. One day my friends are nice and we have a good time together. The next day they change in an instant, or I find out that a friend I shared a secret with told someone else.

Although I trust my mom and dad, some days I am still unsure of who I can *really* trust. What I know for sure, though, is that I can trust You. I can come to You with anything, and You will listen, guide, and help me. Thank You, God, that I can share anything with You. Your Word is true, and I can trust Your promises.

When I feel that no one is trustworthy, remind me that You are. I know that my friends and family are human, just as I am, and they will let me down even if they don't mean to. But You will never fail me, and You will never turn Your back on me. Forgive me when I don't trust You as I should—like when I have to take a big test or go to the dentist and I'm scared. I want to trust and become trustworthy just as You are. Amen.

Your kingdom is an everlasting kingdom,
and your dominion endures through all
generations. The Lord is trustworthy in all
he promises and faithful in all he does.
PSALM 145:13 NIV

The Unseen

My faith in You, Lord, doesn't make sense to a lot of people sometimes. They refuse to believe in something they cannot see. But I see how You have worked in my heart and in the hearts of the people I love and that love You. You've changed us. That couldn't happen on its own. I see little miracles each and every day, and I give You all the credit!

Even though I've never seen You and have never heard Your voice out loud, I trust in the words of the Bible, and I have faith that You are with me.

All I need to do some days is get outside and look at the beauty of Your creation. The sky and the trees and all the living things You created. Life came from You alone, God. I know that with all my heart.

You've filled me with joy because You've given me eternal life. My purpose is to live out my life loving You and pointing others to You. Amen.

Though you have not seen him, you love him; and even though you do not see him now, you believe in him and are filled with an inexpressible and glorious joy, for you are receiving the end result of your faith, the salvation of your souls.
1 PETER 1:8–9 NIV

Temptation

God, temptation is all around me. Whether I am at school or home, I am constantly forced to choose between doing right and doing wrong. Why does it seem easier to do the wrong thing than to resist temptation? I am often tempted in what appears to be small ways, but even the little sins can get out of control. Things like gossiping about others or putting someone down in order to make myself look better. . .

I pray that You will give me power to say no to the things that do not honor or please You, Father. I read of Bible heroes who trusted You and who did not give in to temptation. Their lives were truly blessed. Those who gave in to temptation were given another chance, but they often had to live with really tough consequences for their sins. Help me to choose right over wrong. Be at my side and hold my hand. I think I can withstand temptation if I know that You are always with me, God. Amen.

You are tempted in the same way that everyone else is tempted. But God can be trusted not to let you be tempted too much, and he will show you how to escape from your temptations.
1 Corinthians 10:13 cev

Day 260
Drop It!

I don't like getting my feelings hurt, Lord. It feels awful! And when I get my feelings hurt. . .watch out! Sometimes I hold the person who hurt my feelings in unforgiveness. I refuse to let go of the hurt. I hang on to it like my dog hangs on to his bone! I refuse to give it up. After all, I deserve to feel this way. . .right?

You don't like me to hang on to hurt, Lord. . .for my sake and the sake of the person who hurt me. You want me to let it go, like the dog dropping the bone when his master commands him to.

Help me let go of the offenses. When my feelings are hurt, whisper, "Drop it! Get over it! Let it go!" in my ear. And if I try to hang on to it, remind me that You had every reason to be offended when You sent Jesus to the world and the world rejected Him. You didn't get offended, though. You did just the opposite! You kept loving, kept forgiving, and kept giving. May I learn from Your example, Father! Amen.

Good sense makes one slow to anger,
and it is his glory to overlook an offense.
PROVERBS 19:11 ESV

Loving You

Heavenly Father, I want to love and honor You in everything that I do. I want to follow all of Your commandments and walk in the ways that You have instructed, but I am so easily distracted by things on earth. I find myself focusing more on my schoolwork, friendships, and fun times than I do on following You and keeping Your commandments. I need to remind myself that You are the most important relationship in my life, nothing else compares. I need to remember to talk to You, listen for Your wisdom in my life, and just spend time being quiet in Your presence. Thank You for never growing impatient with me or giving up on me when I forget to talk to You. I know that Your love is perfect and will never cease. No matter what I do, You are always there. Thank You for that assurance and constant love. Amen.

We show our love for God by obeying his commandments, and they are not hard to follow. Every child of God can defeat the world, and our faith is what gives us this victory.
1 John 5:3–4 cev

Cool Stuff

It's important to have cool stuff, Lord. Maybe having the newest gadget or the nicest clothes shouldn't be important to me, but it's hard when all my friends seem to have the latest and trendiest stuff. I don't want to feel left out.

But no matter how great I think something will be, new things get old. Today's trend is tomorrow's toss-away. By next week or next month, that blouse will be old, the shoes will be worn, and there will be some other high-tech gadget on everyone's must-have list.

My parents can't buy me everything I want, Lord. They try to give me the best they can, but even I know the earthly gifts they give me won't last forever.

The gifts You give, though, are perfect. They never wear out. Things like Your love, Your peace, Your joy—those are things money can't buy. They only come from You.

I know the cool stuff I get comes from You. You give me everything I need—and many things I want. Thank You for giving me beautiful gifts, Lord. Help me to be grateful to my parents and to You. Help me remember that every good thing comes from You. Amen.

Every good and perfect gift is from above, coming down from the Father of the heavenly lights.
JAMES 1:17 NIV

What an Awesome Idea!

Heavenly Father, I'm so glad You thought of the idea of church. Some kids think it's boring and just for losers, but I'm glad I know the truth. The church people are my family; they care about me and want to help me live for Your glory and get to heaven someday.

There are different types of churches—some are large, others are small; some like hand-clapping and praise music, and others prefer hymns. But the most important thing is that they proclaim Jesus is Lord and follow the teachings of the Bible.

When I was little, I went to children's church and heard the teachers tell stories from the Bible. Now I'm older and I can listen to teaching without visual aids, but I still remember those exciting scenes that made the Bible seem so real.

Thank You for the church—it's a place of learning and caring. I want to fill my place and be faithful to come and worship and praise. Bless my pastor today, and let me make my church a better place. Amen.

♥

Now you are the body of Christ,
and each one of you is a part of it.
1 CORINTHIANS 12:27 NIV

Day 264
Peace vs. Envy

I never considered *peace* the opposite of *envy*. But the author of Proverbs makes it clear! Help me, Lord, to be content with what I have and where I am in life. Jealousy is like a virus that spreads quickly throughout my entire being when I allow it. First, I find myself thinking about someone else's belongings. I wish I had her designer purse. . .or wouldn't it be great to have a fancy cell phone like his? Then I begin to wish I looked more like someone else. I'd trade this straight mop for those beautiful curls, or vice versa. I compare my family to those of others.

Where does it stop? Envy is not from You, God. I know it is from the devil, who longs to capture my heart and mind with his deceptions. I pray that today You will plant in my heart a deep peace that says, "I'm okay. I look the way God created me to look. I have a good family. And I don't need fancy, expensive things to make me happy."

Peace vs. envy? I choose peace. Amen.

A heart at peace gives life to the body,
but envy rots the bones.
PROVERBS 14:30 NIV

Day 265
Producing Fruit

I want to bear fruit for You, Lord. I imagine two trees—one tree heavy with fruit, so much fruit that it spills over to the ground beneath, and the other tree bearing no fruit at all. Like the fruit-bearing tree, I want to overflow with service to You. I want others to see Jesus in me.

Reveal to me the gifts and abilities You have given me. Help me to know how and where I can serve You best. As I go through my daily life, heavenly Father, point out to me opportunities where I can work for Your kingdom. I want to be Your hands and feet. I want to love others in such a way that they recognize You and come to salvation.

Help me always to remain in close fellowship with You. I know that if I try to do the work on my own, it will be useless, but anything done in Your name will last. You are the vine, Lord. I am a branch. Allow me to produce much fruit for Your glory. Amen.

"Yes, I am the vine; you are the branches.
Those who remain in me, and I in them,
will produce much fruit. For apart
from me you can do nothing."
JOHN 15:5 NLT

Wisdom vs. Foolishness

Wisdom is doing the things I *know* I should do, but foolishness is found in going my own way, not God's. Job tells us that "God alone understands the way to wisdom; he knows where it can be found" (Job 28:23 NLT). I may have knowledge and know a lot, but I can't be wise on my own. Proverbs tells us that wisdom is sweet and brings hope and a bright future (see 24:14 NLT).

Some of my friends don't seem to care about wisdom, but I see all the benefits it brings, and I can already see the results of foolishness in the lives of those around me. I want to have fun, God, but I don't want to be foolish or destroy the hopes and dreams of my life.

I need to learn wisdom, but I also need to learn to value having wisdom, God. It is so easy to just want to follow the crowd or go my own way because not many people follow Your way. Yet You tell us in Proverbs 8:11 that wisdom is far more valuable than rubies and nothing we desire can compare with it.

Give me wisdom, God. Help me avoid being foolish. Amen.

Fear of the LORD is the foundation of true knowledge, but fools despise wisdom and discipline.
PROVERBS 1:7 NLT

Day 267
Cutting Words

I've had it! Father, sometimes I just can't help myself from getting angry—like when a friend makes a rude remark or talks to me with a bad attitude. Or when my parents won't allow me to do something I want to do, or when a girl at school flaunts, boasting about how talented, pretty, or popular she is.

I want to hold my tongue, yet sometimes I don't. I say things that aren't nice, even hurtful to others when someone treats me badly or upsets me. Yet my anger only makes matters worse than they already are.

Please help me curb my anger at those times, Lord. Give me the self-control I need when I want to lash out. Substitute my otherwise cutting, harsh words and responses with words that will calm me and those around me.

I am grateful that You are always kind and loving, even when I'm not. Help me to hold my tongue and answer with kindness as You would do. Amen.

A gentle answer deflects anger,
but harsh words make tempers flare.
PROVERBS 15:1 NLT

Day 268
Doing My Own Thing

It's so hard not to want my own way, Father! Seriously! I just want to ignore what my parents are telling me sometimes and do my own thing. When they give me an instruction, I want to freak out and do something totally opposite. I guess I've been guilty of being really immature sometimes.

You don't like it when I roll my eyes. Or stomp my feet. Or slam my door. Your heart isn't happy when I get demanding and insist I have my own way. You want for me to hear. . .and obey. No arguments. It's not always easy, not when you have a stubborn streak like me!

I know I can be a little rebellious at times, God. Please forgive me for that. I want to be a girl who does what she's told without making a scene. I'm asking You to touch my heart today and get rid of any stubbornness inside of me. The Bible says that I should listen to the adults in my life. Help me to do that with a clean heart, Father. Amen.

Listen, my son, to your father's instruction
and do not forsake your mother's teaching.
They are a garland to grace your head
and a chain to adorn your neck.

PROVERBS 1:8–9 NIV

Keeping My Word

I promised I would babysit, Lord, but my friend invited me to go to the mall with her and a few other friends. I really want to go—I don't want to miss out on the fun! I can just call the family and tell them that I can't babysit after all.

But I'd feel bad, Father—not just because it would put them in a difficult situation, trying to find a replacement on such short notice. But they would have reason to doubt my future promises, and I certainly don't want that!

I want people to know me as a person who is trustworthy—if I give my word, I'll keep my word. But if I begin making promises and then go back on them, I will give them reason to doubt me.

Lord Jesus, I ask for the wisdom to know when to give my word regarding something and when not to. Help me to weigh out the positives and negatives first, before committing to something. And then help me to follow through with my promise, even if it's uncomfortable or difficult for me. In Your name, amen.

Many people claim to be loyal, but it is hard to find a trustworthy person.
PROVERBS 20:6 NCV

Three Things

No matter where I go or how many beginnings and endings I have, I will always go all-out for three things—faith, hope, and love. Faith that You, God, will be with me at all times. Faith that You have a plan for my life. Faith that You will give me the confidence to be and do whatever You want me to be and do.

I will keep the hope that You, Jesus, will give me the power to live this life in Your light. Hope that I will someday be reunited with the loved ones that have gone to heaven before me. Hope that I will one day see Your shining face.

And, even greater than faith and hope, I will live a life of love, reaching out to one and all with the love of Christ, who gives me the strength to do what seems impossible.

With my confident faith, trusting hope, and boundless love, I will live an amazing life, far above the troubles of this world. With these three things, I become one with You. Amen.

But now faith, hope, and love remain;
these three virtues must characterize
our lives. The greatest of these is love.
1 CORINTHIANS 13:13 VOICE

Day 271
Loving Others

Dear God, I don't always find it that easy to love others. You know my thoughts. You know how frustrated I get when I find others annoying or just want to be alone. I need to remember that everyone was created by You and is deserving of respect and love. Especially the people that I find hard to love or who don't love me. When I am around these kinds of people and don't feel like I have any love to give, fill me with Your love—Your constant and everlasting love—because I can't do it alone. Soften my heart toward those who are not easy to love and show me how to serve them with a willing heart. Let love show through my thoughts, words, and actions. Lord, You are the perfect example of love. Let me look to You whenever I am feeling empty and feel like it's impossible to love someone. Amen.

Dear friends, let us continue to love one another,
for love comes from God. Anyone who loves
is a child of God and knows God.
1 JOHN 4:7 NLT

Faith without Works

I love You, God. Of course I love You. If anyone asks me, I'll tell them right away. I love God, and I have faith in Him.

But I'm learning that words aren't enough. I can say I love You, but if my actions don't show that love, what's the point? Words don't mean a thing. Even my thoughts don't mean a whole lot if the way I live my life doesn't match my faith.

If I say God loves everyone, that means I have to love everyone, Lord. Really love them. Sit-by-the-nerdy-kid-who-smells-bad kind of love. If I say I honor You, I have to honor my parents and obey them quickly and with a respectful attitude.

If I say I trust You but try to force things to work out my way, I'm showing I don't really trust You at all. If I say my hope is in You, but I walk around feeling sad all the time, I'm showing I don't really have hope.

Lord, help me to make my faith real. Help me to show, through every action, that I love You, I trust You, I honor You, and my hope is in You. Amen.

Faith by itself, if it does not have works, is dead.
JAMES 2:17 ESV

Day 273
A True Lady

Dear God, I'm beginning to think that boys are kind of wonderful. When I was younger, I thought they were gross and pests and that the world would be better off without them. But my attitude sure has changed a lot lately. I want boys to think I'm pretty and nice to be with. And I'm just realizing that I can act certain ways to get their attention. I guess that's called flirting, and it's actually sort of cool to be able to make boys interested in looking at you. But I know that I have to be careful. There are some kinds of attention that aren't good for me or them.

I need Your wisdom so I will know how to dress myself and how to act around boys. Your Word calls that discretion. I need to know the difference between enjoying being around them and encouraging wrong feelings. I like to be winked at, looked at, and talked to, but help me not to take this too far. I want to be a true lady and not be bold or seductive. Since I belong to You, I want You to be pleased in how I act. Amen.

A beautiful woman who lacks discretion
is like a gold ring in a pig's snout.
PROVERBS 11:22 NLT

Day 274
A Thankful Heart

God, today I am thankful for all that You have given me. Thank You for the people You have put in my life who truly care about me. Thank You for the education I am getting, which will help me to have a job where I can make a difference in the world. Thank You for my friends and family and my home. Thank You for the clothes I wear and the food I eat. I know that all of these things come directly from Your hands.

When I begin to compare myself and what I have or don't have with other people, please remind me to be thankful. Sure, I can always find someone who has more than I do or who appears to have what I want. I have everything I need and much of what I want. There are so many in this world who are in great need. Help me to be content with all that You have blessed me with. Help me always to have a thankful heart. Amen.

Be thankful in all circumstances, for this is God's will for you who belong to Christ Jesus.
1 Thessalonians 5:18 nlt

Kind, Tenderhearted, and Forgiving

This is my prayer today, heavenly Father: that in every difficult situation I face, I would seek out ways to be kind, to have tenderness in my heart toward the other person, and that I'd always be willing to forgive.

Help me to get rid of all the bad thoughts that sometimes come into my head. I know I can hold on to anger a little bit too long. I say things I don't mean sometimes, and I just seem to make a lot of the same mistakes over and over again—especially in my friendships.

You have forgiven me for a lot of things—help me to remember that when the time comes for me to forgive a friend for something in the future. I want to be a kind and tender girl—one who is known for being loving and Christlike. Thanks for giving me Your power and wisdom to guide me in all things. Amen.

Get rid of all bitterness, rage, anger, harsh words, and slander, as well as all types of evil behavior. Instead, be kind to each other, tenderhearted, forgiving one another, just as God through Christ has forgiven you.
EPHESIANS 4:31–32 NLT

Day 276
A Huge Promise

I'm so thankful for Your Word, Lord! It gives me the answers I need for this life. I pray specifically that You would write this verse in Philippians on my heart and bring it to mind every single time I worry. Just saying this verse out loud brings a sense of peace and calm to my heart.

Help me not to worry, but to pray when I feel nervous or anxious about anything. Help me to share my feelings with You as I feel them instead of holding them inside and getting even more stressed. I want to be thankful instead of stressful!

When I give thanks to You instead of worrying, a very powerful thing happens that You've promised right here in Your Word: You'll give me peace! A peace that doesn't really make sense to anyone else but me. And You'll guard my heart and my mind as I live in You, Jesus. What a huge promise! Amen.

♥

Don't worry about anything; instead, pray about everything. Tell God what you need, and thank him for all he has done. Then you will experience God's peace, which exceeds anything we can understand. His peace will guard your hearts and minds as you live in Christ Jesus.
PHILIPPIANS 4:6–7 NLT

Radiant

Lord, I heard someone describe a gorgeous actress as radiant. She was beautiful in her sparkly dress, but she was also with a good-looking actor, and she looked really happy. She looked like the kind of person I could be friends with, the kind of person who would be nice to a stranger. I think that's what radiant means. . .it's a kind of pretty that comes from being happy and full of love.

I've known some really pretty girls who don't look happy at all. They're mean and sullen, and honestly, most people are afraid to be around them. Those girls may have some skin-deep beauty, but they're not radiant.

Lord, I want to look nice on the outside, but I don't want it to stop there. I want to shine with happiness and kindness and gentleness. I don't want people to be afraid of me or worry that I'll hurt their feelings. I want to have the kind of beauty that draws people to me. . . and I know that kind of beauty comes from being like You. Help me to be radiant today, Lord. Amen.

Those who look to him are radiant.
PSALM 34:5 NIV

Saving for Eternity

Please help me to be a good steward, Father. I know that means taking good care of the finances and things You've blessed me with here on earth. I want to use my money and my blessings to honor You. I'm giving a portion of all my money to You, and I'm also saving money for the future and for that special thing I really want to buy.

I know You're okay with all of that, but I also know that You don't want me to put all my hope in earthly treasures and lots of money. If I treasure any "thing" too much here on earth, it will take a hold of my heart in ways that aren't pleasing to You.

Help me to store up treasures in heaven! The kind of treasures I'll receive in eternity for loving and serving You with all my heart. For doing things for others without recognition and without expecting anything in return.

"Do not store up for yourselves treasures on earth, where moths and vermin destroy, and where thieves break in and steal. But store up for yourselves treasures in heaven, where moths and vermin do not destroy, and where thieves do not break in and steal. For where your treasure is, there your heart will be also."
MATTHEW 6:19–21 NIV

Making Wise Decisions

Lord Jesus, I need Your help in making wise choices.

Friends invite me over and want to watch a movie that I think my parents wouldn't approve of. Does it really matter if I watch it just this one time?

I can check this book out of the library on my own library card, and even though it doesn't appear to be totally pure, couldn't I just skip over those parts?

There's a new TV show that I've heard a lot about. I'm home by myself, and I don't get scared *that* easily. Why shouldn't I go ahead and watch it?

Although I have these internal "debates," I really know the answer, Father. Your Spirit tells me to avoid things I know are wrong, whether there is anyone around or not. It's so much easier to just do it, especially if I think I'll be made fun of if I don't. But obedience is much more important than trying to fit in. I want to make You happy, Jesus, no matter what that means to my reputation. Amen.

Our only goal is to please God. . .because we must all stand before Christ to be judged. Each of us will receive what we should get—good or bad—for the things we did in the earthly body.
2 CORINTHIANS 5:9–10 NCV

Okay in My Own Skin

God, can I admit something? Sometimes I'm not okay in my own skin. I'm really grateful You created me, and I know You want me to relax and be myself, but sometimes I just wish I could look like someone else or have the talents of someone else. It's not always easy to be me! I see all of my flaws—every bump and every wrinkle. I wonder if other girls see themselves this way too. Do we all wish we could be different? Are we all uncomfortable in our skin?

Father, remind me that You created me in Your image. When You look at me, You don't compare me to others. I know Your Word says that You're crazy about me, just the way I am right now—with every freckle, every messy hair, every flaw. Before I was ever born, You knew exactly what I would be like, and the Bible says that all of Your works are wonderful. Amen.

For you created my inmost being; you knit me together in my mother's womb. I praise you because I am fearfully and wonderfully made; your works are wonderful, I know that full well.
PSALM 139:13–14 NIV

If I Had My Way

Lord, I don't understand why I can't have my way about certain things. The things I want aren't bad things; I want to have fun and be happy and have friends and have cool stuff. Is that wrong? I'm not trying to be selfish. But I don't understand why some things—good things—don't always go my way.

If I had my way, Lord, every day would be filled with smiles and laughter and happiness. Every day would be like a fairy tale, with birds singing and little animals dancing, and the bad would lose and the good would win. What's wrong with that, Lord?

Then again, if there were no bad things, no disappointments in life, I guess I wouldn't really appreciate the good things. If all I ever knew were happiness and singing birds and rainbows, I'd have nothing to compare them to. I might not appreciate life's joys as much if I didn't have some disappointments along the way.

Help me today to be grateful for even the hard things in life. I know they help me grow. They give me wisdom and bring me to a deeper appreciation of Your goodness. Amen.

Consider it pure joy, my brothers and sisters, whenever you face trials of many kinds.
JAMES 1:2 NIV

Wisdom vs. Knowledge

I'm learning so much in school, Lord; sometimes I feel like I can't fit it all in. I love learning new things. When I think of all the stuff I need to know, though—math, science, spelling, reading skills, writing skills—I feel overwhelmed.

All that stuff is knowledge, Lord, and it's good to have all the knowledge I can have. Knowledge will help me be successful in whatever I do in life. But if there's one thing that's more important than knowledge, it's wisdom. Knowledge is all about facts and figures and knowing how to do things. Wisdom is about making good life choices.

Knowledge may teach me how to build a house, but wisdom will teach me to have a happy home. Knowledge may teach me the right medicines to use to clean a scratch on my knee, but wisdom shows me how to heal a heart.

Father, I need Your wisdom. I don't always know what to say or do or how to respond to my circumstances. Give me Your wisdom so I can make good choices for my life. Amen.

♥

If any of you lacks wisdom, you should ask God, who gives generously to all without finding fault, and it will be given to you.
JAMES 1:5 NIV

My Best Friend

Friends are fun. Thank You for the friends in my life, Lord. My girlfriends make school a lot more enjoyable, and they listen when I have a problem. We do crazy things together, and we have the best day ever! We feel more like sisters sometimes.

But I have some days when I feel like my friends don't understand or they can't relate to how I feel. Other "friends" are pretend because they talk behind my back and change friendships constantly. Although I realize that different friends will come and go in my life, help me to appreciate my true friends. Not only that, help me to become a dependable friend others can trust.

You, Father, are my very best friend. You are always with me to listen and help. You understand me even when I don't understand myself! You accept me as I am but love me too much to leave me that way. Jesus, thank You for being a true friend. Amen.

Some friends are fun to be with,
but a true friend can be better than a brother.
PROVERBS 18:24 ERV

A Secret Place

Lord, I know there is a secret place where nothing can touch me—it is in You. In Your presence, I am safe. Leaning against You, all my troubles roll off my shoulders.

When I am confident in You, totally trusting You for everything, all Your promises come true. Your angels lift me up, protecting and saving me from dangers I don't even see. I find comfort under Your enormous and all-powerful wings. Nothing is able to frighten me—neither tests, nor strangers, nor harmful words. When I am facing any kind of challenge, I merely call on You and You come immediately to my rescue.

I know nothing can get to me because You are my constant shield. As long as I am living in You, Your courage, Your peace, and Your power are mine. Thank You for being such an awesome God. Amen.

♥

He who dwells in the secret place of the Most High shall remain stable and fixed under the shadow of the Almighty [Whose power no foe can withstand]. I will say of the Lord, He is my Refuge and my Fortress, my God; on Him I lean and rely, and in Him I [confidently] trust!
PSALM 91:1–2 AMPC

Day 285
Always

Lord, it is so comforting to know that You will always love me and be kind to me. That is not true of people. Everyone will let me down at some point. Even my closest relatives and friends are not perfect. Your love is not like any love in this world. It is constant and forever. You have sought me out as Your child and drawn me to Yourself. You have caught me up in the kindest hug ever, and You will never walk away, never fail, and never disappoint.

God, I know that Your will is what is best for me. Help me to trust You as doors close in my life, that You will open the ones I need to journey through at just the right time. You are my loving heavenly Father who will never let me go. Thank You, God, for loving me with an everlasting love and blessing me with Your sweet kindness. It is only through Christ that I can come into Your presence. I am so thankful that we will be together always. Amen.

The LORD appeared to us in the past, saying:
"I have loved you with an everlasting love;
I have drawn you with unfailing kindness."
JEREMIAH 31:3 NIV

Day 286
Dream Big!

If You know the plans You have for me (Jeremiah 29:11), then how do I know what they are? Everyone tells me that You have a plan and purpose for my life, but what if I somehow miss it?

Maybe it is too soon to know exactly what my future will look like, God, but I know that I want to choose Your plans over mine. I dream of doing great things one day—of being successful and living a life that counts for something. I need Your help to do that. I have so much yet to discover and am still trying to figure it all out. What am I good at? What are my gifts?

Your Word tells me, "God has given each of you a gift from his great variety of spiritual gifts. Use them well to serve one another" (1 Peter 4:10 NLT). That means that I have gifts and strengths and talents too! Help me to figure out what those are and how to use them in ways that will honor You most. Amen.

God began doing a good work in you, and I am sure he will continue it until it is finished when Jesus Christ comes again.
PHILIPPIANS 1:6 NCV

Constructive Criticism

When someone criticizes me, it hurts. Sometimes even my closest friends have said things that have embarrassed me or made me angry, even though deep inside I knew their comments were true.

Everyone has faults; I have plenty myself, I know. Yet when my parents or family point out my flaws, it makes me upset and uncomfortable. How do I handle that, Lord? I know You don't want me to lash out in anger or ignore them and stomp to my room to pout. It's just hard to know what to do.

Father, when my mom or dad tells me something about myself that I know is true and I need to change, give me the humility and ability to change my reaction to their comments. Change me. Help me to receive the truth and take it to You in prayer instead of allowing my hurt feelings to cause resentment.

I know my parents love me and want what's best for me, just like You do, Lord. When they give me constructive criticism, it is only to help me become a better person, a better Christian. Help me to know the difference and act accordingly. Thank You, Lord, for loving and accepting me just as I am but caring too much to leave me that way. Amen.

Remember what you are taught,
and listen carefully to words of knowledge.
PROVERBS 23:12 NCV

Day 288
God Is Awake

I have a lot on my heart tonight, Lord Jesus. My heart is heavy about many things, and I know You're the only one who can help. You're the only one who can control any of this. You see every side of the story—even when it doesn't make any sense to me.

I'm tired, Lord. I can't fix this. The only thing I can do is pray to You and trust that You will have Your way in this situation.

There are things in my life—and in this world today— that hurt my heart. I'm coming to You because You tell me to come to You with my burdens and You will give me rest (Matthew 11:28). I am weary and burdened. This stuff feels heavy on my shoulders. Will You give me peace and rest tonight?

Thank You that I can go to sleep knowing that You're watching over everything and that You're still awake, taking care of it all. Amen.

♥

My help comes from the LORD, who made heaven and earth! He will not let you stumble; the one who watches over you will not slumber. Indeed, he who watches over Israel never slumbers or sleeps. The LORD himself watches over you!
PSALM 121:2–5 NLT

A Princess, for Real?

Am I really Your princess, heavenly Father?

You have told me that I need to believe that You died for me and rose again from the dead. As difficult as it is to think of the suffering You went through for me, I *do* believe that You loved me so much that You died and rose again. I have asked You to forgive me for the sins that sent You to the cross for me.

You not only call me Your princess, though; You call me an "heir of God's glory." I'm an heir who gets to share in Your glory! I can only imagine how awesome Your glory is, but that You have chosen me, as Your follower, to share in that is beyond comprehension.

Thank You for saving me from eternal death and for preparing a special place for me in Your heaven. I want to live my life for You out of a heart full of love. And one day, I will finally get to see the face of my eternal King. Thank You, Jesus! Amen.

But to all who believed him and accepted him,
he gave the right to become children of God.
JOHN 1:12 NLT

Tearing Up the Picture

Do You ever have a hard time forgiving people, God? I do. When people hurt me, I don't want to forgive. Sometimes I just want to be mad or get even. It's almost like I take a picture of what the person did to me and stare at it all day long. I can't get it out of my mind, no matter how hard I try. The more I stare at it, the more offended I get!

Your Word says that I should be quick to forgive because You were quick to forgive me. I guess that forgiving someone is kind of like tearing up the picture of what they did and throwing it in the trash. When I do that—when I let go of it—You are free to heal my heart.

Yesterday is in the past. Today is what matters. Lord, You've already forgiven me for the sins I committed yesterday. Show me how to forgive others who have hurt me the same way You've already forgiven me. Amen.

"Come now, let's settle this," says the Lord.
"Though your sins are like scarlet, I will make
them as white as snow. Though they are red
like crimson, I will make them as white as wool."
ISAIAH 1:18 NLT

Day 291
Daily Faith

Lord, walking with You in faith is harder than it sounds. When people in Sunday school talk about faith, it sounds so easy; I just have to trust You to take care of everything, and You will. But I'm finding it is much harder to have constant faith in You than I thought. My first instinct is to have faith in my friends or in myself, or I constantly worry and don't trust You to provide for my needs. Lord, You have been so faithful to me in the past. Help me to remember that when I'm struggling with something new and I don't turn to You or have faith that You can handle a situation. Thank You for always being faithful to me; I want to be faithful to You too. Amen.

It is written in the Scriptures, "I believed, so I spoke." Our faith is like this too. We believe, and so we speak. God raised the Lord Jesus from the dead, and we know that God will also raise us with Jesus. God will bring us together with you, and we will stand before him.

2 CORINTHIANS 4:13–14 NCV

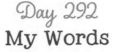

Day 292
My Words

Lord, I have the hardest time controlling my tongue. I want to be nice. I want to be the kind of person who encourages people with their words, who is always kind, always respectful. And sometimes I am all those things. But other times, I'm just plain mean.

Sometimes I can be sweet to a person's face, but say unkind things about them behind their backs. Sometimes I can pray and tell You how much I love You, God, and five minutes later I'll be saying or thinking something mean about one of Your children. I know that's wrong.

Help me to love others with my words, whether it's to their faces or behind their backs. I want to be the kind of person others can count on, the kind of person others feel safe around. Before I say anything unkind, help me to ask myself if the thing I'm saying is true. Even if it's true, is it kind? Is it necessary to say that thing?

Give me wisdom, and help me control my tongue in a way that honors You. Amen.

Out of the same mouth come praise and cursing.
My brothers and sisters, this should not be.
JAMES 3:10 NIV

Day 293
Patience

Lord, waiting doesn't come easily for me. Sometimes I just want to hurry and grow up—to get the newest cell phone, to be able to date and drive and make my own decisions. Maybe it's because I've grown up in an "instant society," but when things don't happen immediately, I start to get a little anxious. Fast-food, fast information, fast communication—everything seems to be at our fingertips.

Patience is a virtue—something to value and pursue. Your Word tells me that patience is a fruit of Your Spirit (Galatians 5:22). I guess that means I can't do it very well on my own—I need Your help! Patience is waiting for the right time for everything and trusting You for the result, not myself.

Help me develop patience, God, to live fully in the "right now" of my life. To enjoy what I have and to be content to wait for what is ahead. I know You have the future under control and that You want what is best for me. Slow me down, Lord, and help me to appreciate all that You have for me now. Amen.

But let patience have its perfect work, that you may be perfect and complete, lacking nothing.
JAMES 1:4 NKJV

Day 294
God in My Corner

I love the amazing stories in Your Bible, Father God, especially where You show how powerful You are! There's one story about huge armies coming to fight King Jehoshaphat. Instead of totally panicking, Jehoshaphat ran right to You and asked for help. And boy, did You give it! After lots of prayer and praise from Jehoshaphat and his people, You made the enemy armies attack each other! Not one hair on the heads of the Israelites was harmed. Not only that, but they ended up with all their enemies' treasures!

When I come up against trouble, it's so comforting to know I have such a powerful God in my corner. All I need to do is come to You, pray, stand firm, and watch You fight the battles. Thank God You are with me in every way every day. Keep opening my eyes to Your presence as I go through this life with courage and hope while walking Your path and singing Your praise. Amen.

"You will not even need to fight. Take your positions; then stand still and watch the Lord's victory. He is with you. . . . Do not be afraid or discouraged. Go out against them tomorrow, for the Lord is with you!"
2 Chronicles 20:17 NLT

The New Me

Heavenly Father, I want to please You with my life. When I am around other Christians, I get so excited about Your Word. I love to sing praise and worship songs. But I find that when I am with non-Christians, it is harder to stand strong in my beliefs.

There are all kinds of choices out there, Father, and some of them frighten me. The older I get, the more I will be faced with temptations regarding things that are not pleasing to You. Help me, Lord, to turn from sin. Make me sensitive to the still, small voice of the Holy Spirit whom You have sent to counsel me.

I know that as a human being, it is impossible for me to be perfect. I am a sinner who has been saved by grace through faith in Your Son, Jesus. In Your power, I can make right choices and resist the urge to sin against You. Strengthen me, I pray. Help me to stand out in the crowd as a follower of Christ. Amen.

Those who are God's children do not continue sinning, because the new life from God remains in them. They are not able to go on sinning, because they have become children of God.
1 JOHN 3:9 NCV

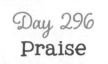

Day 296
Praise

God, the psalms are filled with reasons to praise You. I know that You alone deserve all praise and honor. What surprises me is what praising *You* can do for *me*! Praising You brings hope and joy into my life. It brings confidence and trust.

Praising You is just telling it like it is. You are wonderful and mighty. You are beyond my human understanding. When I praise You, my attitude about everything else changes! When I sing worship songs or tell others or remind myself of who You are and what You have done for me, my heart feels glad and it changes my perspective.

Even when circumstances in my life are hard to deal with, You stick with me and comfort me and help me out of trouble. Those times when life is difficult, help me to remember that You never change, nor does Your love for me. You are steadfast and faithful. I can depend on You because You never fail, even if others in my life do. Always remind me of who You are and what You have done for me. Amen.

Let all that I am praise the LORD; may I never forget the good things he does for me.
PSALM 103:2 NLT

Shop with Me, Lord

Fashions? I do like them! I enjoy shopping for new clothes, and sometimes I get carried away. Yet I want to please You, Father, in every area of my life, and dressing modestly is one of those areas.

Some girls flaunt their bodies with clothes that are too revealing. I ask that You help me resist those kinds of choices. I want to reflect Your Spirit inside and out, and the clothing I choose is a part of that.

Sometimes it's hard to avoid trendy clothing or brand names. So when I shop, I ask that You help me make the right choices to look attractive without giving in to the latest fashions that might be inappropriate for me to wear. I don't want a designer label to lure me into buying something that might be impressive but impractical.

I know I spend a lot of time on how I look and the clothes I wear, so I ask for You to guide me more toward serving You and less toward caring far too much about how I appear on the exterior.

I pray for a pure heart and proper attire that mirrors who a believer is inside and out. Amen.

Women, the same goes for you: dress properly, modestly, and appropriately. Don't get carried away in grooming your hair or seek beauty in glittering gold, pearls, or expensive clothes.
1 TIMOTHY 2:9 VOICE

God Is Sovereign

I've given You my heart, Lord. And Your Word tells me that nothing can separate me from Your love. You promise to always be with me—leading and guiding me closer to You and Your plans for my life.

Open my eyes to see You working in my life and the lives of those around me. Open my ears to hear what You want to say to me through Your Word. Open my heart to fully experience the relationship that You long to have with me.

Remind me that nothing can get in the way of Your love for me. You are sovereign, which means You have ultimate power and authority over everyone and everything. Don't allow me to be fooled into thinking anyone else has control over me or this world. You are God, and I'm not. And neither is anyone else.

Thank You for caring so much for me. Amen.

For I am convinced that neither death nor life,
neither angels nor demons, neither the present
nor the future, nor any powers, neither height
nor depth, nor anything else in all creation,
will be able to separate us from the love
of God that is in Christ Jesus our Lord.
ROMANS 8:38–39 NIV

Day 299
Socially Acceptable

I'm so thankful for technology, Lord. Some days I think I could never live without it. But then I realize I need to keep it in perspective. If I'm not careful, it could become an idol to me—something that takes priority over You. And I would never want to be guilty of that!

Father, please guard my thoughts, my eyes, and my hands as I am online or on my phone. I love to have conversations with my friends, but sometimes it can get close to gossiping as we chat. If I can't say—or type—anything nice about someone, I shouldn't say it at all.

Please keep me pure as I view and post photos. I know what's right and what's wrong, but sometimes, in the name of a joke, the line can be crossed.

Help me to remember, Jesus, that I need to choose my words carefully and to only hit SEND or ENTER if I know what I've typed will please You. Once the words are "out there," I can never get them back. Please give me wisdom. Amen.

Let the words of my mouth and the meditation
of my heart be acceptable in your sight,
O LORD, my rock and my redeemer.
PSALM 19:14 ESV

Day 300
Good Fruit

Thanks for creating fruit, Lord! It tastes so good and is so good for me; I don't know many people who don't like at least one kind of fruit. You tell me about spiritual fruit in Your Word, and it makes a lot of sense to me. A heart that is pleasing to You produces good, yummy fruit. A heart that is not following You produces sour, gross fruit.

Please fill me with the kind of spiritual fruit that tastes good to others and is good for me. The Bible says there is no law against being loving or joyful or full of peace, patience, kindness, goodness, faithfulness, gentleness, and self-control. I'm not going to get into trouble with anybody for showing that kind of fruit! It's healthy for my body and my soul and will lead me closer in my relationship with You, God. Amen.

But the Holy Spirit produces this kind of fruit in our lives: love, joy, peace, patience, kindness, goodness, faithfulness, gentleness, and self-control. There is no law against these things! . . . Since we are living by the Spirit, let us follow the Spirit's leading in every part of our lives.
GALATIANS 5:22–23, 25 NLT

Day 301
Being Beautiful

Heavenly Father, a lot of the time I feel like the world is telling me that being beautiful is the most important thing about being a girl, and I really want to be beautiful; that's a natural desire. But I know there are so many things that are more important, and lasting, than whether or not everyone thinks I'm pretty. Help me to remember that it is more important to be kind, loving, and walking with You daily than it is to be pretty. You designed me, and You find me beautiful even if I don't have perfect hair or blemish-free skin. You don't judge me based on how I look, so I don't want to judge anyone else based on their physical appearance, even if it's an easy thing to do. Please help me to love the body and the face that You have given me rather than focusing on everything that I want to change. May all of my thoughts, words, and actions be glorifying to You. Amen.

Charm can be deceiving, and beauty fades
away, but a woman who honors the
Lord deserves to be praised.
PROVERBS 31:30 CEV

Day 302
Pray First

Sometimes I forget to pray, Lord. I know I'm praying right now, but many times when I'm faced with something hard, I try to figure things out on my own. I try to solve the problem the way I think it should be solved, or I go to my friends for advice, or I just get frustrated and give up. And then...after everything else has failed...I might remember to pray.

It's not wrong to try to figure things out on my own, Lord. But I should pray first. It's not wrong to seek advice from friends, as long as I'm seeking Your advice first. Prayer should be my first option, not my last resort. If I talk to You, I might avoid the frustration that comes with trying all the wrong things first.

There will always be troubles in my life, Lord. Every day I'll be faced with circumstances I don't know how to handle, problems I don't know how to fix. When these situations come up, help me remember to talk to You first before trying anything else. Amen.

Is anyone among you in trouble?
Let them pray.
JAMES 5:13 NIV

Day 303
Far Deeper Love

Sometimes, Lord, people are just so hard to figure out. I think my friends are mad at me—but I have no idea why. Was it something I said or did? Or was it something I *didn't* say or do? All I know is that I feel like an outcast.

And although this appears to be a bad situation, it reminds me that even if my friends desert me, I will always have You. The love You have for me and show to me is far deeper than any love a human can express. Your tender care, Your hopeful promises, Your daily blessings overwhelm me.

With that in mind, I know nothing anyone says or does can really hurt me. So, Lord, lift my burdened heart. Clear the confusion from my mind. Give me bright hope for tomorrow. Fill me with the light of Your love, and allow it to shine through me so that I can learn to love others—even when they seem not to love me.

No one has ever seen God. But if we love
each other, God lives in us, and his love
is brought to full expression in us.
1 JOHN 4:12 NLT

A Glimpse of God

I know that I am a work in progress, Lord. Every day I am changing more and more into the woman I will someday be. In the meantime, though, I know I need to treat my body right. That means not going on starvation diets or eating ten Oreos every night but finding a happy medium. It means getting exercise every day, whether by taking up a sport at school or playing tennis or walking in the park.

Help me, Lord, to remember that my body really isn't my own—it's Yours. Give me the wisdom to treat it right. Help me to feed my mind, body, and spirit in such a way that when people see me, they will catch a glimpse of You. Amen.

Didn't you realize that your body is a sacred place, the place of the Holy Spirit? Don't you see that you can't live however you please, squandering what God paid such a high price for? The physical part of you is not some piece of property belonging to the spiritual part of you. God owns the whole works. So let people see God in and through your body.
1 CORINTHIANS 6:19–20 MSG

Day 305
Fitting In

I guess everyone feels like this sometimes, God. It seems as if lately I feel like this a *lot*. I just don't "fit in." I want to blend in and be like everyone else. But I stick out like a sore thumb! Just when I think I have the style figured out, it changes. I never seem to say the right thing. I can be so awkward at times. My parents say it's just my age, but I don't think this is something I will outgrow. I am just always sort of in between. I'm not the least popular, but certainly not the most popular. I do have some friends. I just never feel like I am part of the "right" crowd.

I guess as a Christian, I am not really meant to fit in down here on this earth. I am supposed to be different. Just help me, God, to find Christian friends that I can relate to and enjoy. If they are already in my life, help me to recognize their great value. I need to just rest in Your arms right now, Lord. I belong to You. You are where I "fit in." Amen.

But our citizenship is in heaven. And we eagerly await a Savior from there, the Lord Jesus Christ.
PHILIPPIANS 3:20 NIV

So Many Dumb Moments

Lord, I never knew that growing up meant I would have so many dumb moments. Many times I say things that later I think were stupid. And I worry that everyone will think I'm pitiful.

I want my friends to think I'm cool, not dumb. But when I tell something funny, not many kids laugh, and when I think something is great, someone else always mentions something better. My parents tell me to be myself, but that doesn't seem to be good enough. When I'm at home, I'm okay, but when I get out with friends at school or church, I usually feel like I blow it.

I remember hearing about Moses, who had trouble speaking in public and was nervous about doing what You asked, yet You were with him. So I'm asking You to help me be the person You made me to be. I want to learn to be comfortable in a group and to be able to communicate well, but I don't want to constantly worry about what others think. I'm depending on You to help me get it right as I grow and learn. Amen.

My mouth will speak words of wisdom.
PSALM 49:3 NIV

Day 307
It's about Time!

It seems I just don't have enough time—between school, home, and after-school activities, homework and chores, the day passes too quickly. Time flies, especially when I connect with Instagram and Twitter. Unlike working on homework, which takes a lot of time and effort, texting is fast, easy, and fun!

With everything that I do, Lord, I ask that You help me manage my time better. I don't want to waste too much of it doing the things that are simple and easy. I realize that in order to grow in You, I must spend time reading the scriptures and pray daily. But usually other "things" distract me from the important matters of the heart.

Father, I confess that I spend too much time doing time-consuming activities that are unproductive. Please place a check in my spirit when I'm tempted to spend too much time on entertainment in place of spending quality time with You.

Your Word says there is a time for everything. I thank You that You have made enough hours in the day for me to accomplish everything I need to do, want to do, and should do. But I know it's about time that I give You time before anything or anyone else. Amen.

There is a time for everything.
ECCLESIASTES 3:1 NCV

Day 308
A Brand-New Heart

God, I've messed up so many times. Here I am coming to You again with the same thing. Will You forgive me yet again? Your Word says that You do, and I'm so grateful! But please help me not to take advantage of the fact that You are a forgiving and gracious God!

I'm embarrassed by what I've done, and I come to You humbly, asking for You to help me be a better person and not mess up so much. I know I'll never be perfect until I'm in heaven with You...but I really want to do the best I can for You down here! Help me to make this right with the people that I've hurt in the process of my sin. I'm ashamed by my actions. Please help me do the right thing!

No matter what I do, it seems You are always waiting for me with open arms and an overflowing heart. I love You, Lord. Thank You for wiping my slate clean and giving me a brand-new heart to start fresh again. Amen.

But you, Lord, are a compassionate
and gracious God, slow to anger,
abounding in love and faithfulness.
PSALM 86:15 NIV

Go Against the Flow

I really want to be accepted by my friends, Jesus. Most of the time there isn't a problem—I'm not confronted with temptation very often.

But once in a while I'm tempted to do something I know is wrong. It's even more difficult when a whole group of them do it—I don't want to look like a freak! And I tell myself it probably is harmless.

But You have told me not to go with the crowd if they're doing something wrong. That feels like walking against the current of a raging river sometimes. I can get swept away with peer pressure, or I can take a stand and act in a way pleasing to You. You don't promise that it will be an easy decision, but You do promise to be with me and to give me a way out.

Lord Jesus, please give me the strength to choose what's right, even if a bunch of people give in to temptation and do what's wrong. In Your name, amen.

Don't copy the behavior and customs of this world, but let God transform you into a new person by changing the way you think. Then you will learn to know God's will for you, which is good and pleasing and perfect.

ROMANS 12:2 NLT

Day 310
A Little Respect

Thank You, Lord, for the people You've placed in my life—parents, grandparents, aunts, uncles, teachers, leaders at my church. . .all of the wonderful people You've blessed me with. Show me how to show them respect, God. They totally deserve it! You've placed these special grown-ups in my life, and I'm so blessed to know them. I want to treat them with politeness and great manners, with courtesy and kindness. Someday I'm going to be a grown-up, and I will want kids to treat me that way!

When I get frustrated with the adults in my life, please guard my tongue and help me to respond in a way that brings honor. May my actions reflect a respectful heart. And Lord, when I see other kids treating grown-ups disrespectfully, give me the courage to let them know that what they're doing is wrong. Maybe I can set a good example by showing them how they should treat their elders. I'm going to try, for sure! Amen.

Never speak harshly to an older man, but appeal to him respectfully as you would to your own father. Talk to younger men as you would to your own brothers. Treat older women as you would your mother, and treat younger women with all purity as you would your own sisters.

1 Timothy 5:1–2 nlt

When It's Hard to Trust

Dear God, You have never abandoned or betrayed me. You have always loved me, even when I seem unlovable. You even died for my sins. I want to have complete trust in You because of these reasons and for all the ways that You have provided for me. You will never let me down; I know that You are always looking out for me. But sometimes it's hard to trust because I've been hurt or let down by others in the past, and even though I know You are perfect and cannot let me down, I still find it hard to trust You with all of my problems and doubts. Please be patient with me when I struggle and doubt. Show me how to completely trust You with everything in my life, Lord. There are so many examples of people in scripture who completely trusted You, like Esther when she married the king who was persecuting her people. If she could trust You in that situation, then I should be able to trust You with everything in my life. Thank You for Your patience with me, Lord, as I learn to trust You with everything in my life. Amen.

"God is the one who saves me; I will trust him and not be afraid. The LORD, the LORD gives me strength and makes me sing. He has saved me."

ISAIAH 12:2 NCV

Day 312
A Good Name

I want to have a good reputation, Lord. When people think of me, I want them to think good things. But a good reputation has to be earned. It's the result of many wise decisions over a long period of time. A good reputation is the result of good character.

One important quality I need, if I want people to think well of me, is love. All my words need to be loving. All my actions need to be loving. People need to feel safe around me, like they are wanted and accepted. Some people are easier to love than others, Lord. Help me to love everyone the way You love them.

Another important quality is faithfulness. I need to do what I say I'll do. I need to remain true to my friends and family, even when I feel betrayed. I need to remain true to my values, even when it would be easier to toss them aside.

Help me to consistently live the qualities that will give me a good name, Lord. When people think of me, I want them to think of You. Amen.

Let love and faithfulness never leave you....
Then you will win favor and a good name
in the sight of God and man.
PROVERBS 3:3–4 NIV

Day 313
Level Failed

Father, I feel like I really messed up. . .again. I keep making mistakes and don't know if I'll ever measure up.

In the Bible, I find that there are many people who failed. Eve ate the fruit You told her not to, and then she convinced Adam to sin as well. Sarah laughed when You promised that she'd have a baby in her old age. Potiphar's wife lied and got Joseph thrown into jail. Miriam spoke against her brother, Moses, and was struck with leprosy. And Job's wife told him to "curse God and die!" (Job 2:9 NIV). Not the most shining examples of godly women!

But You included these stories so we can know that even if we fail, good can come from it. We can be restored to a right relationship with You, and we can also serve as reminders to other young women that God can even use our failures.

Thank You for not expecting me to be perfect. I put pressure on myself to be perfect, but that is my expectation, not Yours. You only ask that I obey and walk in Your way, and when I do fail, that I repent and move on, continuing to follow You. Amen.

My flesh and my heart may fail, but God is the strength of my heart and my portion forever.
PSALM 73:26 NIV

Day 314
The Sunny Side

Lord, there seems to be so much trouble in this world. Different countries are fighting wars. Children in many places have no food or water, no school to go to, not even toys to play with. And then there are the earthquakes, tornadoes, and hurricanes destroying houses and crops! All this bad news tends to weigh me down.

Help me, Father God, to fill my mind with good thoughts, things that are beautiful, not ugly. Things I can cheer for, not cry about. That doesn't mean I will ignore all the bad stuff. It's just that I'm going to focus on what's *good* in this world—not on what's evil. I want to live in Your light, not the dark. So help me, Lord, to walk and stay on the sunny side of the street each and every day, to say prayers for those who need them, and to praise You for all Your wonders here on earth. Amen.

♥

Fix your thoughts on what is true, and honorable, and right, and pure, and lovely, and admirable. Think about things that are excellent and worthy of praise. Keep putting into practice all you learned and received from me—everything you heard from me and saw me doing. Then the God of peace will be with you.
PHILIPPIANS 4:8–9 NLT

Calm the Storms

Calm the storms in my heart, Lord Jesus. When You were on this earth, You simply spoke, and the strong winds died down. The waves became still. You amazed the men who witnessed this. Amaze me with that same power in my life, please. It seems my whole world is crashing down. I can't count on some of the people I trusted most. Everything is changing. And yet, I feel so stuck in this in-between age. Not a little kid, but not old enough to be independent.

Lord, You know about storms and struggles. You lived here in this world. You were betrayed by some of those who were Your closest friends. You never even had a home to call Your own. In fact, You were arrested for no wrongdoing and then crucified. Thank You for coming to earth and living as a man. It helps me to know that You understand my heartache. Calm my storms, Lord, and if some of them must continue for now, just hold me. I feel safe with You, Jesus. Amen.

Jesus answered, "Why are you afraid? You don't have enough faith." Then Jesus got up and gave a command to the wind and the waves, and it became completely calm. The men were amazed and said, "What kind of man is this? Even the wind and the waves obey him!"
MATTHEW 8:26–27 NCV

The Words I Say

God, sometimes I use words I know I shouldn't. They just slip out. James 3:8–10 says that no one can tame the tongue. Blessing and cursing come out of the same mouth, and that shouldn't be the case. I know I need to watch what I say, but how do I do that?

It is so easy to pick up words that other people use. I don't want to mimic others; I want to be like You! The best way to do that is to put into my heart and mind what is good and to choose not to use words that are ugly. Like everything else that is hard to do, it takes discipline—and I need Your help!

Jesus told His disciples that the words we speak come from our hearts (Matthew 15:18). That's where change starts. The things I think about, look at, the people I hang out with, whatever I focus on—that is what will show up in my speech.

Help me focus on You, Your Word, and what pleases You, God. Amen.

The heart of the godly thinks carefully
before speaking; the mouth of the
wicked overflows with evil words.
PROVERBS 15:28 NLT

I Want to Obey!

Thank You, Father, for my family. I love my parents, and I want to honor and obey them; but sometimes I don't… like when my mom tells me to empty the dishwasher, clean my room, finish my homework, or do something I'd rather not do at the moment. My parents often ask me to do things that are inconvenient or just poor timing. At least that's the way I feel. Maybe I'm in the middle of texting a friend or watching Netflix. At those times, it's especially hard for me to obey.

I guess it's similar to obeying You. After all, how can I learn to obey You if it's so difficult for me to obey my parents? Forgive me, Lord. Please help me to remember that You gave me great parents and grandparents to lead, teach, and raise me according to Your will and ways.

When I am tempted to talk back, Lord, help me to hold my tongue; when obedience is hard, give me the strength to do what I know is right. I want to honor and respect my parents by honoring and showing You respect in all that I say and do. Amen.

Children, obey your parents because you belong to the Lord, for this is the right thing to do. "Honor your father and mother."
EPHESIANS 6:1–2 NLT

Day 318
A Fragile Jar

Father, help me to remember who is in control of my life. I try to take control back from You sometimes, but then I'm reminded that I'm just a fragile jar that You have chosen to make Your home in. You are the source of the light in my heart.

If others notice great things about me, give me the courage to tell them the story of You. And that it is only through You that I'm able to accomplish anything of value. Help me remember that You are the one who gives me power and strength in this life. Anything I do is about You and for You. I really want that to be true of me, God. I want You to be honored in my life.

Please cleanse me of any pride in my heart. I want this life to be about Your love shining through me and not about me and what I can do on my own.

♥

We now have this light shining in our hearts, but we ourselves are like fragile clay jars containing this great treasure. This makes it clear that our great power is from God, not from ourselves.
2 CORINTHIANS 4:7 NLT

Choosing Friends

Is it wrong, Lord, to want to fit in? Is it wrong to want to be part of the crowd? Sometimes I find myself saying and doing things I know aren't right, just so I can be more popular. I want people to accept me. I want them to like me. I'm not proud of it, but some days I feel like I'd do just about anything to be popular.

But deep down, I know that if people don't like me unless I go against what I know is right, they're not really my friends. Those kinds of friends will only lead me into trouble.

It's such a hard place to be, Lord. I don't want to be that kid in the corner who doesn't have any friends. I also don't want to behave badly just to be popular. Either way, I know I'll be unhappy.

Help me choose my friends wisely, Lord. Send people into my life who will encourage me to make good decisions, who will encourage me to honor You. And help me to be that kind of friend to others as well. Amen.

The righteous choose their friends carefully,
but the way of the wicked leads them astray.
PROVERBS 12:26 NIV

Day 320
Mean Girls

Ooo, some girls can be so mean, Lord! They act like they're better than everyone else. They play mean tricks on people. They lie and do other things that are just plain bad. Whenever I'm around girls who act like this, I want to be mean right back. But that's not what You ask me to do. Your girls—and I'm one of them—are not supposed to repay evil with evil. Instead, the Bible says we are to repay evil with good. We are supposed to bless those who hurt us.

It's not always easy to repay evil with good, but I'm going to give it my best shot, Father! The next time those mean girls start acting up, I'm going to turn the other cheek. No, it won't be easy, but maybe they will learn a lesson from me. And maybe, if I really pray about it, I can win them over with Your love. I'm going to try anyway! Amen.

Don't repay evil for evil. Don't retaliate with insults when people insult you. Instead, pay them back with a blessing. That is what God has called you to do, and he will grant you his blessing.
1 PETER 3:9 NLT

My Hope Is in You

Dear Lord, thank You for giving me hope. I have so many desires and dreams for my life, and I need to remember to give all of my hopes to You because You will provide for me. I know that even though I may not understand why certain things happen, You do. And since my hope rests in You, I will not be let down. I sometimes place my hope in places I shouldn't, like my friends, or my parents, or myself and my own abilities. Whenever I do this, I am always let down and disappointed by myself and others. Lord, please remind me that real hope and assurance come only from You. Teach me to look to You for everything I need and to expect great things from You. Even though it is so easy for me to get discouraged and forget to hope, I need Your reminders in my life. Amen.

In him our hearts rejoice, for we trust in his holy name. Let your unfailing love surround us, LORD, for our hope is in you alone.
PSALM 33:21–22 NLT

Day 322
A Great Big "Thank You!"

Bad days? I know I will sometimes have them, Father—probably more often than I'd like. Everything from horrible hairstyles to fights with my best friends, skinned knees to a broken heart. . .I've experienced them all. When I have a bad day, I usually end up feeling sorry for myself and having a private pity party in my room—shut away from anyone and everyone who cares about me. But worst of all, I end up shutting You out as well. I'm so sorry for that, God.

Even though I can't control the things that can and will go wrong, please help me to remember that I *can* control my reaction to those things. So the next time I have a bad day, Father God, I'm asking for You to send me a little reminder of everything that's *wonderful* in my life: my family, my pet, my bedroom that's decorated just the way I like it, my very best friends. . .and most of all, *You*!

I'm sending up a great big "thank You!" for everything good in my life. Amen.

Always give thanks for all things to God the Father in the name of our Lord Jesus Christ.
EPHESIANS 5:20 NLV

Day 323
Seeing Isn't Believing

I like to see things, God, so faith is a little difficult for me. In science, we learn about observation and the importance of it in investigation. But I can't observe You. Some people say that means You don't exist; they say we should only believe what we can experience with our five senses. But I can't ignore the things I've been taught and the verses I've heard and the feeling deep inside me that tells me You are real.

I can't see You or touch You, but I have felt You in my soul, speaking to me. I have seen You working through my parents and my pastor and others. I have felt peace when I've prayed and forgiveness when I've asked for it. I have seen You answer prayers.

So I just want to say today that I believe in You even though I can't see You. I'm still learning about faith and what it means, but I know You're going to be there for me every day of my life. Thank You for sending Your Son to die for my sins so that I can have a relationship with You. In Jesus' name, amen.

Then Jesus told him, "You believe because you
have seen me. Blessed are those who
believe without seeing me."
JOHN 20:29 NLT

Day 324
Blessings to Bless Others

Some people call me a "do-gooder," Father, as if that's a bad thing. And sometimes, Lord, that can be hard to take. But I know how You would like me to behave. And to tell You the truth, God, I feel better and happier when I am doing the things You would have me do.

So, Lord, give me the energy to continue doing good things. Show me all the ways I can help or work with the people in my Sunday school class, youth group, and church. Keep me from getting so busy with school, sports, games, and activities that I don't have extra time to do things for others.

Thank You for giving me the simple task, time, or talent to serve people in a way that shows them what You are all about and draws them closer to You. Keep energizing me as I use my blessings to bless others, starting with my family at home and church.

So let's not allow ourselves to get fatigued doing good. At the right time we will harvest a good crop if we don't give up, or quit. Right now, therefore, every time we get the chance, let us work for the benefit of all, starting with the people closest to us in the community of faith.

GALATIANS 6:9 MSG

Day 325
Everything I Need

You want to bless Your children, Father. I see a glimpse of this type of love when I look at earthly parents who give their kids good "stuff." Just as a generous, caring mom or dad gives his or her child food, clothing, and shelter, You provide this and so much more for Your children. You provide Christian friends for me to enjoy time with and grow alongside. You have provided a school and a church for me. My home and family are direct gifts from Your hands. You have given me everything I have—even my abilities and talents. Every good and perfect gift truly comes from You, my heavenly Father.

I love to read the stories in the Bible where You really came through and provided just what was needed. I know that You will continue to meet my needs as I get older. You are the great provider, and for this I am humbly thankful. When I begin to worry about tomorrow, calm my fears. Remind me, Lord, that You have it all under control. Amen.

♥

And my God will supply all your needs according to His riches in glory in Christ Jesus. Now to our God and Father be the glory forever and ever. Amen.
PHILIPPIANS 4:19–20 NASB

Day 326
Mean Girls

God, Your Word tells me to love those who hate me—but I'm not so sure I can do that! Other people can be so mean. How do I love someone who doesn't love me back? Even those I thought were my friends are not always kind.

I know You faced bullies, Jesus—those who crucified You were not only cruel, they enjoyed hurting You. Sometimes I think people like to see others suffer. I want to respond the way You did—with love—but I need Your help! It is not always easy to look on others with compassion and understanding.

Lord, please help me to see others as You do—to understand that often those who hurt us are in pain themselves. That does not make their actions right, but it might help me to know that they may be striking out because they are hurting, not just because they want to hurt me. Thank You that when others were unkind to You, You loved them in spite of themselves, just as You love me! Amen.

"Love your enemies! Do good to them. Lend to them without expecting to be repaid. Then your reward from heaven will be very great, and you will truly be acting as children of the Most High."
LUKE 6:35 NLT

Day 327
Never Alone

Sometimes I feel alone, even with family and friends around me. I don't get it. Maybe I feel as if they don't really understand or care about me. I'm not sure.

I dislike it when I get into one of those moods. But I do have them. I have days when I think that no one likes me, and I really want and need their love or attention. But instead I feel rejected. . .even if it makes no sense!

At those times, Father, remind me that You are always with me—that I'm never alone. Before I even speak one word in prayer, You are there. You understand how I feel and why I feel that way. Thank You for being so close and caring so much.

You promised to never leave or reject me no matter what. So help me to remember that even when I feel alone, I'm not. You're at my side at all times. Amen.

Where could I go to escape from your Spirit or from your sight? If I were to climb up to the highest heavens, you would be there. If I were to dig down to the world of the dead you would also be there. Suppose I had wings like the dawning day and flew across the ocean. Even then your powerful arm would guide and protect me.
PSALM 139:7–10 CEV

Shining Through

I'm having another bad hair day, Lord. No matter what I do, it looks either messy, flat, or out of control. And my wardrobe is another issue. I feel it definitely needs some refreshing.

Although I want to look my best, there are some days when I just can't seem to get it together. That's when I am reminded that no matter how fat or skinny, small or tall, fashionable or unfashionable I feel, that's not what's important. As long as I'm neat and clean, You are happy with how I look on the outside, whether I'm in old jeans and a T-shirt with my hair in pigtails or wearing a new outfit and the latest hairstyle. Instead, Your concern is that I am beautiful on the *inside*.

Lord, help me to spend more time on my inner rather than outer beauty—for my inner beauty will glow forever. Thank You for loving me for what is within my heart. Remind my unique and special self to shine for You—and You alone.

Don't depend on things like fancy hairdos or gold jewelry or expensive clothes to make you look beautiful. Be beautiful in your heart by being gentle and quiet. This kind of beauty will last, and God considers it very special.
1 PETER 3:3–4 CEV

Day 329
Got Attitude?

I know I can have a bad attitude sometimes, Lord, but everybody does, right? We all have bad days and need to vent. Sometimes I holler at the person who is the closest to me. Other times I just give the "silent treatment." I'm even too angry for words.

It isn't fair when I have to clean up someone else's mess! And it's infuriating when I get blamed for something I didn't do. I try to defend myself (and sometimes say a bit more than that!) so that the world knows I'm innocent and mad that I was blamed.

But that reaction isn't the right one, Father. You didn't defend Yourself when You had every right to do that. I want to learn from Your example. The next time I'm accused of something I didn't do, please remind me to count to ten. I also ask for grace to do what I'm asked anyway, even if it wasn't a result of anything I did. I need Your strength, Lord. Amen.

Do all things without grumbling or disputing,
that you may be blameless and innocent,
children of God without blemish in the
midst of a crooked and twisted generation,
among whom you shine as lights in the world.
PHILIPPIANS 2:14–15 ESV

Day 330
Taking Time to Talk

Spending time with You is a privilege, God! It's so awesome to think that the One who created everything— the earth, people, all of nature—wants to hang out with me. How cool is that? I love that You want to hear about my day and about all the things I'm going through. I'm also glad that You listen when I'm upset and help me when I'm struggling. Best of all, I love that I can pray for other people and You take the time to answer my prayers.

The Bible says that You listen when I talk to You. You take me seriously. And I can ask You tough questions. Nothing's too hard for You, Lord! If I ask You to heal my grandmother's backache, You can do it! If I ask You to protect my dad while he's on his way to work, You can do that too. You're definitely the most powerful friend I've ever had. Just one more reason why I love hanging out with You! I'm always amazed by You! Amen.

And we are confident that he hears us whenever we ask for anything that pleases him. And since we know he hears us when we make our requests, we also know that he will give us what we ask for.
1 JOHN 5:14–15 NLT

Security in God

Lord, I get so afraid sometimes. I constantly worry about things like tornadoes, my parents getting sick, or something happening to my friends. I worry about things that I have no control over. Whenever I start to worry, I need to remember that You are in control and will keep me safe. Remind me to tell You all of my fears and give them over to You, for only You can comfort me during those times. I know that no matter how ridiculous my fears seem, You will understand them and will not make fun of me. It is so easy to forget that You are in control and that I am in the palm of Your hand at all times. Thank You for all the times that You remind me of Your love and protection, and help me to trust You with every worry and fear that I have. Help me in the future when I struggle with fear and feel insecure. Amen.

♥

You need not be afraid of sudden disaster or the destruction that comes upon the wicked, for the Lord is your security. He will keep your foot from being caught in a trap.

PROVERBS 3:25–26 NLT

Day 332
Just a Kid

I'm just a kid, Lord. There's not much I can do to make a difference in this world. Right?

But I want to make a difference. I want to live my life in a way that points other people to You. Whether it's in school or at home or in my neighborhood, I want people to look at me and feel like they know You better. I want them to feel loved and accepted and respected, the way You love and accept and respect them.

Some people may look down on me because of my young age, Lord, but I know You don't. I know You've put me here for a reason and that purpose doesn't begin later. My purpose doesn't start when I graduate or when I get a job or get married or have children. My purpose here on earth began the day I was born. Before that, even.

Lord, help me to live out Your purpose for me every single day, starting today. Amen.

Don't let anyone look down on you because you are young, but set an example for the believers in speech, in conduct, in love, in faith and in purity.
1 TIMOTHY 4:12 NIV

Day 333
Have Patience

Waiting is hard, Lord. Whether it's waiting in line, waiting for my turn in the bathroom, or waiting to be older so I can do more stuff, I just don't like having to wait. It may be selfish, but I want what I want when I want it. . .which is right now!

You said patience is a good thing. I know the only way I can practice patience is by having to wait for things or by having to put up with things I don't like very much.

You also said it's important to be happy through whatever is going on in our lives right now. Not that we have to like everything, but You want us to keep trusting You and not freak out about stuff. It's called "being content."

It's funny, Lord. I want people to be patient with me, but I'm not always patient with others. I want the people in my life to be calm and gentle no matter the circumstance, but I don't always act that way myself. Help me to have patience and be content, no matter what happens in my life today. Amen.

For I have learned to be content
whatever the circumstances.
PHILIPPIANS 4:11 NIV

Day 334
Strength in All Things

When I forget to include You in my day, Father God, I end up feeling tired, uncertain, and sometimes a bit frightened. So help me to remember to take strength from You and arm myself with Your Word before I start each new day—I know that I can be ready for anyone and anything when I am staying close to You.

Right now I am going to take time to rest in Your gentle care, Lord, knowing that You will give me the spiritual, mental, and physical muscle to do all I need to do. Focused on You, I can pass that test, kick that ball, do my homework, understand Your Word, and more—I can do all that You have created me to do. No matter what challenges or troubles I face, You will help me get through them. Thank You for giving me the strength and power to become what You want me to be—a girl with her eyes on You. Amen.

♥

I have strength for all things in Christ Who empowers me [I am ready for anything and equal to anything through Him Who infuses inner strength into me].
PHILIPPIANS 4:13 AMPC

Security in the Lord

Heavenly Father, I don't mean to worry. It's really a bad habit! Sometimes I let the things of this world overwhelm me. I worry about school, grades, friends, and the future. I worry about what I wear and how my hair looks. I worry about not fitting in with the "right" groups. And to think, I am just a kid! How many more things must adults have to add to the list? I sometimes sense that adults in my life are worried about how to provide or what choices to make.

I don't want to be a worrier now or in the future when I'm a grown-up. Your Word tells me not to worry about tomorrow because every day has enough concerns of its own. I know I don't need to look into an unknown future with fear. Take the burden of my worries, Lord. I lay my concerns at Your feet. In You and You alone I find security. Give me strength to face each day as it comes, and remind me that You've got my back! Thank You, God. Amen.

And when I was burdened with worries, you comforted me and made me feel secure.

PSALM 94:19 CEV

Can You Hear Me Now, God?

God, sometimes I pray and it feels like You aren't answering, like maybe You aren't even listening. Those are times when I feel frustrated and alone. I admit that I may even doubt that You are there, or worse, that You are, but You won't help me.

The truth is, even though I *feel* like You aren't there— You are! I remember that Jesus said, "I will never leave you; I will never abandon you" (Hebrews 13:5 NCV). That means that on those days when I feel as if my prayers don't rise higher than the ceiling, You *are* still there. You care about my problems; You are listening and ready to help me. You are working in my life. You may be testing me, challenging me to grow more dependent on You. Or maybe You are waiting to answer, helping me develop patience.

Lord, I can't understand all the reasons why sometimes it seems like You are slow to act, but I want to learn to trust You. To believe that You love me and care about what happens in my life. Help me to know that You are always there for me. Amen.

"And be sure of this: I am with you always,
even to the end of the age."
MATTHEW 28:20 NLT

True Friendship

What does true friendship look like? Loyalty and honesty are important to relationships. Real friends talk about more than just surface things. They keep confidences and don't tell others your secrets. A true friend is someone you can trust. They are dependable and try not to let you down. When they do, they aren't afraid to say they are sorry and made a mistake.

Am I that kind of friend to others, God? Can they count on me to be there for them, to care about their circumstances of life? Sometimes I can be selfish and want to look to everyone else to meet my needs. You tell us in Philippians 2:3 to think of others as better than ourselves. That means putting others first, caring about their needs above my own.

In order to have a friend, I know I must be a friend. Help me be a true friend, God. One who loves no matter what. Help me be loyal and honest and think about others before myself. Amen.

♥

Dear friends, let us continue to love one another,
for love comes from God. Anyone who loves
is a child of God and knows God.
1 John 4:7 nlt

God Is Faithful

Father, I'm making Psalm 89 my prayer today: "I will sing of the LORD's unfailing love forever! Young and old will hear of your faithfulness. Your unfailing love will last forever. Your faithfulness is as enduring as the heavens. . . . All heaven will praise your great wonders, LORD; myriads of angels will praise you for your faithfulness. For who in all of heaven can compare with the LORD? What mightiest angel is anything like the LORD? The highest angelic powers stand in awe of God. He is far more awesome than all who surround his throne. O LORD God of Heaven's Armies! Where is there anyone as mighty as you, O LORD? You are entirely faithful" (Psalm 89:1–8 NLT).

These verses give me the perspective I need on things, Father. You are faithful. You've always been faithful, and You'll always be faithful. So I know You will continue to be faithful to me. You will guard me and keep me from being destroyed by evil. Thank You, heavenly Father! Amen.

But the Lord is faithful; he will strengthen you and guard you from the evil one. . . . May the Lord lead your hearts into a full understanding and expression of the love of God and the patient endurance that comes from Christ.
2 THESSALONIANS 3:3, 5 NLT

Day 339
That's What I Think

Dear Father, thank You for not condemning me for the thoughts I think. You know all about me—the horrible thoughts I have—and yet You can still forgive me and love me. I would be beyond humiliated if my thoughts were shown on a screen for everyone else to see. And I'm certain I would be so hurt by others' thoughts of me too.

I want to train my mind, God, so that I can think of things that are of You—things that are good and pure. Not everything in this world is good or pure, but my reaction to it can be. I can refuse to compromise on what I watch and read. I can choose friends who will speak in an acceptable way. I can talk kindly to my family (that one can be the hardest!). But all of those decisions take some mental preparation.

Fill my mind with Your love and goodness so that my thoughts reflect Your ways. In Your name, amen.

So letting your sinful nature control your mind leads to death. But letting the Spirit control your mind leads to life and peace.
ROMANS 8:6 NLT

Day 340
Choices, Choices!

Wow, there are a lot of choices to make in life! When I go to the grocery store with my mom or dad, I see thousands and thousands of products to buy. It's hard to know which one to get because there are so many, so I just stand and stare at them all, confused!

The same thing is true with other choices in my life. I face them every day—at school, at home, and when I'm hanging out with my friends. I want to make the right ones every time, but it's so overwhelming sometimes. I get confused and don't know what to do.

Can You help me make better choices, Father? Help me choose better things to watch on television, better ways to respond when people hurt my feelings, and better foods that are healthier for my body. Help me to choose love over hate, joy over anger, and peace over arguing. I need Your help, Lord! Whenever I start to make a bad choice, whisper the words "Make a better choice!" in my ear. Amen.

"Watch and pray so that you will not fall
into temptation. The spirit is willing,
but the flesh is weak."
MATTHEW 26:41 NIV

Day 341
Your Creation

Dear Lord, I am so grateful for the beautiful world You created. For the blue sky, the rainy days, the green hills, and the sandy beaches. I'm thankful for the vast variety of animals that You created, from the cute puppy to the terrifying hammerhead shark; they were all designed by You! And each creation is a reminder of the care that You take when You create. If I ever doubt Your presence, all I need to do is look outside and be reminded of Your care. Show me ways that I can help take care of Your creation and love all the creatures You have created. When I'm feeling small and insignificant, remind me of how You provide for the birds of the air and how much more You provide for me. Amen.

♥

"And to all the beasts of the earth and all the birds in the sky and all the creatures that move along the ground—everything that has the breath of life in it— I give every green plant for food." And it was so.

GENESIS 1:30 NIV

Staying Close

I don't know what to say to sad people, Lord. Sometimes bad things happen to people around me, and I don't know how to help them. Maybe someone they love dies. Maybe their parents are getting a divorce. Or maybe they're just sad because they didn't make the team. I want to make things better for them, Lord, but I can't.

I've tried talking, but I never know the right thing to say. I often end up saying too much or saying something that makes it worse. I've tried giving gifts and doing things for them, but no matter what I do, I usually can't fix the problem.

I guess the best thing I can do, sometimes, is just be there. Just stay close and let them know I care. You said You are close to the brokenhearted, Lord. Maybe that's what I should do too. Just stay close.

Help me to know how to comfort hurting people, Lord. Give me wisdom to know when to speak and when to remain quiet, when to act and when to just stay close. Amen.

The Lord is close to the brokenhearted
and saves those who are crushed in spirit.
PSALM 34:18 NIV

Day 343
Under My Skin

Dear God, I've been thinking about my moods. Sometimes I feel cool and confident, and then other times I am so uptight. I wish I could stay calm all the time, but I can't. Of course, there are things that make my day bad—my hair doing weird things, my face breaking out, or my mom not understanding me—but then there are days when my day just feels ugly without a reason. And when I feel ugly inside, I usually act ugly. I don't blame my family and friends for not liking me then; I don't like myself very much either when I'm like that.

I'm asking You now, God, to help me deal with these moods. You can give me the strength to act nicely even when I feel yucky or when things are going wrong all day.

I try to dress myself nicely, but I'm asking You today to help me dress my spirit well too. I want what's under my skin, the real me, to be attractive. Please help me think about what I do and say so that the beauty of Jesus will be seen in me. Amen.

Let everything you say be good and helpful,
so that your words will be an encouragement
to those who hear them.
EPHESIANS 4:29 NLT

A Daughter's Faith

Lord, I love the Bible story about the woman of great faith who reached out to Jesus. She had been bleeding for many years and had seen many doctors. When she heard about Your Son, she had one goal—to touch Him. She knew in her heart that Jesus could heal her. She had such faith! And with that faith she reached out, touched His clothes, and was healed *immediately*! All her suffering was over!

Then Jesus, knowing His power had gone out from Him, looked around to see who had touched Him. When the woman confessed that she had done it, Jesus had amazing words for her: "Daughter, your faith has healed you. Go in peace and be freed from your suffering" (Mark 5:34 NIV).

May those words be the ones I take right into my heart. May the idea that at any time I can reach out, touch You, and be better be planted firmly in my brain. May Christ say to me, "Daughter, your faith has healed you." Amen.

♥

When she heard about Jesus, she came up behind him in the crowd and touched his cloak, because she thought, "If I just touch his clothes, I will be healed." Immediately her bleeding stopped and she felt in her body that she was freed from her suffering.

MARK 5:27–29 NIV

Day 345
Lullaby from God

I remember when I was just a very little girl, I used to love to hear a lullaby. Whether someone sang it in order to get me to sleep or I heard it on a wind-up toy of some type, it was always so sweet and soothing. I find it amazing, God, that Your Word says You "rejoice over me with singing." The God of the universe taking time out of His busy schedule to sing a lullaby over me! Now that is an awesome thought!

Father, thank You for loving me the way you do—without condition, regardless of the circumstances, and even when I am not as faithful as I should be. You are sovereign and all-knowing. You are a Mighty Warrior who saves Your children. You created me, and You are delighted with me as Your daughter. You even sing over me in joy. I must be pretty special to You, Lord. I am one blessed girl. Amen.

"The Lord your God is with you, the Mighty Warrior
who saves. He will take great delight in you;
in his love he will no longer rebuke you,
but will rejoice over you with singing."
ZEPHANIAH 3:17 NIV

Day 346
Loving Others

I like hanging around people who encourage me, who like me and tell me so! It's easy to get focused on just my friends and forget to include others. What if my friends don't accept them or they don't fit in? Or what if I reach out to someone and they reject my offer of friendship? It's hard to move beyond my own circle of close friends and look for those who may need encouragement themselves.

Jesus told us to love our enemies (Luke 6:27), and The Message says to "let them bring out the best in you." If we are to bless those who curse us and pray for those who hurt us, shouldn't it be easy then to simply reach out to someone who needs a friend?

Give me courage to act kindly and reach out and love others, God. Help me to be a friend to someone who might not have many friends or needs some encouragement of their own today. Amen.

Don't just pretend to love others. Really love them. Hate what is wrong. Hold tightly to what is good. Love each other with genuine affection, and take delight in honoring each other.
ROMANS 12:9–10 NLT

I'm Ready for Change!

Change is difficult. I don't like or understand some of the changes in my life—like why my moods shift so much, or why problems cause conflicts at home or school, or why a friend is friendly one day then seems to ignore me the next.

Habits are hard to change too, because I'm so used to doing the same things. I like to watch my favorite TV shows, and I enjoy texting friends. If I can't do those things, it bothers me. Then I get crabby, and that's not good for me or my family.

I know that change is a part of life, and I need to adjust to those changes. But how? Only You can help me, Father. Your Word tells me that some changes are good for me, and I shouldn't shun them. Help me to make the changes in my life that will bring inner growth. As my body changes and grows outside, I pray that my spirit will change and grow inside. Amen.

And our faces are not covered. We all show the Lord's glory, and we are being changed to be like him. This change in us brings more and more glory, which comes from the Lord.
2 Corinthians 3:18 erv

Ambassadors for God

Dear God, I've learned that reconciliation means making things right with someone and that You've done that with the whole world through Jesus. You sent Your Son to bear all of our sins on His body on the cross so that we might die to sins and live for You (1 Peter 2:24).

But we still have to do our part, Lord. I get that. You want us to accept Your free gift and allow Christ to make His home in our hearts, being the director of every aspect of our lives.

Now that I understand that, I know You've given me the job of telling it to the rest of the people in my life. I'm Your ambassador—Your representative. You're actually using me to tell the world the truth about You!

That is a great responsibility that I don't take lightly, Lord. Help me to share with others boldly and in a way that shows love and light. Amen.

♥

For God was in Christ, reconciling the world to himself, no longer counting people's sins against them. And he gave us this wonderful message of reconciliation. So we are Christ's ambassadors; God is making his appeal through us. We speak for Christ when we plead, "Come back to God!"

2 CORINTHIANS 5:19–20 NLT

Day 349
Healthy Habits

What is wrong with me, God? I just crave foods I shouldn't eat! French fries and chocolate are not the greatest things for me to eat, I know, but they taste so good! Still, both of them are bad for me. So what should I do? I feel guilty when I eat something that's not healthy, but I get really depressed thinking that maybe I'll have to eat salads forever.

My request today, Father, is that You will help me to be balanced. I want to be able to stop with a few fries or bites of chocolate. I know that You want me to be healthy, and yet You don't ask me to always deprive myself in order to please You. Help me know how to do this right, please. And help me remember to feed my soul with healthy food—Your Word—so I won't be tempted by the junk food of this world. Amen.

How sweet are your words to my taste,
sweeter than honey to my mouth!
PSALM 119:103 NIV

Don't Be a Nosy-Poke!

Heavenly Father, I'm so curious sometimes. I want to know everything that's going on around me, every single detail. In other words, I get in other people's business! I nose in where I don't belong. I don't mean to be a nosy-poke. I guess I'm just curious. Sometimes my "curiosity" gets me in trouble. I go too far. The Bible calls these people "busybodies." Ouch! Guess I've been one at times.

Father, help me to remember that people have boundaries. They need their own space, just like I need mine! I'm not supposed to get in their business unless they ask me to, and even then I just need to pray for them, not try to fix their problems.

And Lord, when people get in my business—when the nosy-pokes in my life try to weasel their way into my problems and situations—help me to respond graciously. I want to be kind and loving, even when the busybodies try to fix my problems.

Here's my new motto, Father: "Say no to nosiness!" With Your help, I can do it! Amen.

♥

For we hear that some among you are leading an undisciplined life, doing no work at all, but acting like busybodies.

2 THESSALONIANS 3:11 NASB

Forgiving Others

Heavenly Father, help me to forgive my friends and family when they hurt me. It is so hard to forgive someone when I am hurting and upset or when I feel rejected and alone. Sometimes I would rather just walk away and never forgive the person I am angry at, but I know that is not what You would want me to do. Soften my heart to them and help me to forgive them just as You have forgiven me and everyone else in the world. Lord, You are the perfect example of forgiveness. You have not only forgiven the entire world, You have forgiven people who openly hated You and crucified You on the cross. Help me to look to Your example when I don't want to forgive someone and remember how many times You have forgiven me. Thank You for Your never-ending patience with me. Amen.

"If you forgive those who sin against you,
your heavenly Father will forgive you.
But if you refuse to forgive others,
your Father will not forgive your sins."

MATTHEW 6:14–15 NLT

Day 352
Getting Even

People can be mean sometimes, Lord. Especially kids my age. It seems like the meaner someone is, the more others want to be their friend. The meaner the person, the more popular they are.

When people are mean, Lord, I want to be meaner. I want to plot and plan and get even and show that person that they'd better not mess with me again. But I know that's not Your way, Lord.

When I react with anger, the other person will just react in a bigger, uglier way, and then it will be my turn to outdo them, and the drama will grow and grow until everyone is miserable.

No, I don't need to repay evil for evil. I need to do the right, good, kind, loving, caring thing no matter what. I need to live out Your love, even when those around me don't.

Especially when those around me don't.

Lord, give me wisdom, and help me do what's right even when I am hurt. I want to repay evil with good so others can see what a difference You make in our lives. Amen.

Do not repay anyone evil for evil. Be careful to
do what is right in the eyes of everyone.
ROMANS 12:17 NIV

More Than Background

I'm wanting to download more music, God, but I think I need to ask Your opinion first. It's easy just to choose whatever my friends say is good; still, I don't think that's the best way to do it. Some kids say it doesn't really matter, that the words aren't really that important. But I know that, for me, music is more than background. I catch myself humming the tunes and singing the words even when I'm not actually aware that I'm doing it. Some songs make me feel happy and ready to take on the world; other songs make me think about all the problems in my life. And some songs make me feel angry toward my parents and teachers.

I want to honor You in the music I listen to because I know it affects my attitude and my relationship with You. Please help me make good choices in the music I download and listen to and memorize. I want You to be Lord over this area of my life too. In Jesus' name, amen.

And whatever you do, whether in word or deed, do it all in the name of the Lord Jesus, giving thanks to God the Father through him.
COLOSSIANS 3:17 NIV

Day 354
Ask, Seek, Knock

Lord, I have a lot of questions. I don't know what the future holds for me, and I'm a little too curious sometimes! I get worried and anxious that I'm going to mess up and miss out on Your great plans for me. Will You help me stay on the right path?

Your Word promises that Your plans for me are good. And I believe You! I really do want to follow You with all of my heart. Please keep my eyes and ears from evil, and firmly set Your Word in my heart. Thank You for the Holy Spirit living inside my heart who guides me and reminds me of everything I need to know each day.

I'm Yours, Lord. Help me seek after You all the days of my life and not worry so much about the future. You've got this, God. And I trust Your faithfulness!

"Ask, and it will be given to you; seek, and you will find; knock, and it will be opened to you. For everyone who asks receives, and the one who seeks finds, and to the one who knocks it will be opened."

MATTHEW 7:7–8 ESV

Day 355
The Love of Money

I have expensive tastes, Lord. I notice nice things. Whether it's an expensive cell phone or the latest designer fashions, it is just so hard not to want, want, want! I know that my walk with You is so much more important than *things*, but I need help, Father. It's not easy for me to be content with what I have. I find myself making lists of things I would like to have as gifts for my next birthday. I save up all my money for things that really aren't necessary.

Help me, Lord, to be happy with the things I already have and not be constantly working toward acquiring that "next thing." I know I am so blessed and that many people do not even have necessities such as food and water. Give me eyes to see beyond the glitter and glamour of the things of my world to the hurt of theirs. Help me to use my resources to help others. You are what lasts, God. You will never leave me. I want You more than I want the things of this world. Amen.

💜

Don't fall in love with money. Be satisfied with what
you have. The Lord has promised that he
will not leave us or desert us.
HEBREWS 13:5 CEV

Starting Over

God, I mess up sometimes—actually, I mess up a lot! I think about giving up trying to do things the right way because I fail so often. But You don't want me to give up! You offer me forgiveness again and again—every time I need it.

The apostle Paul talks about his struggle with sin and doing what's right in Romans 7. I'm like him—I want to do what's right, but I don't always succeed. When I don't get it right, I need to start over. The first step is coming to You, God, and telling You all about it. You understand and forgive. To me that is amazing, especially when I find myself doing the same wrong thing over and over again.

Confessing is just agreeing You are right, that Your way is the best, the only way. Help me when I fail to turn to You. Thank You for forgiving me and giving me another chance. Amen.

♥

If we claim that we're free of sin, we're only fooling ourselves. A claim like that is errant nonsense. On the other hand, if we admit our sins—make a clean breast of them—he won't let us down; he'll be true to himself. He'll forgive our sins and purge us of all wrongdoing.
1 John 1:8–9 msg

More about You,
Less about Me!

Sometimes I think too much. *What should I wear today? Did someone notice when I tripped over my book bag at school? Should I cut my hair? Will I ever understand math? I hope no one saw the hole in my T-shirt!*

Lord, sometimes I think more about myself than I think about You. I don't mean to; it just happens. My mind fills up with things, and I get wrapped up in my own thoughts. But I know it's not always about me; it's about You and others. Please help me to remember that when my thoughts run out of control. Remind me to pray for my friends and family and the problems they face every day.

I know it's selfish to think too much about myself. I'm glad You're not like that. You are unselfish, loving, and considerate. I want to be like You, Father. The Bible says that You are always thinking about me. That is so awesome and incredible. I want to think of You the same way. When too many of my thoughts are about me, help me to become Christlike and redirect my thoughts more toward You and others. Amen.

How precious to me are your thoughts, God!
How vast is the sum of them! Were I to count
them, they would outnumber the grains of
sand—when I awake, I am still with you.
PSALM 139:17–18 NIV

Day 358

Friendships That Honor God

God, I'm glad You gave me a lot of advice about the kind of friends I should have. In Proverbs, You tell me not to make friends with people who are always angry and are known by their temper. In 1 Corinthians, You tell me to keep away from people that call themselves Christians but have secret sins they keep doing over and over again. You remind me again and again not to gossip because it ruins friendships. And so many other great verses about the kind of people I should hang out with. You've given me so many words of wisdom to follow, and I thank You for that!

I pray that You would provide me with a strong group of friends that will encourage me in my walk with You, Lord. Friends that I can pray with and depend on for help when I need it. And friends that I can have good, clean fun with, Lord! Let our conversations be full of our love for You and for each other. Let us be good examples to other kids and younger friends and family members. Amen.

Don't befriend angry people or associate with hot-tempered people, or you will learn to be like them and endanger your soul.
PROVERBS 22:24–25 NLT

Day 359
Renew My Strength

I'm tired, Lord. Sometimes trying to do the right thing and to please those around me just wears me out. I love my parents and want to honor them, but it's also important to me to fit in with my friends. It's hard to keep everyone happy! School is hard work—keeping up with all the assignments and homework. And then there are extracurricular activities and thinking about high school. . .and college or my future job. . .

I know I am young, but life is hard! I am thankful that my hope is in You, heavenly Father. I can come to You and spend time with You. I can find refreshment for my weary soul when I pray and read Your Word. My strength is renewed when I just rest in You and let You have the worries of my day. Thank You for giving me the endurance that I need to live life one day at a time. I love You, Lord. Amen.

Even youths grow tired and weary, and young men stumble and fall; but those who hope in the LORD will renew their strength. They will soar on wings like eagles; they will run and not grow weary, they will walk and not be faint.
ISAIAH 40:30–31 NIV

Staying Active in Church

God, I love being part of my church. It's the perfect place to grow up! Talk about great people! I'm surrounded on every side.

Help me to find a way to fit in so that my gifts can be used. I want to worship with my friends and family, but I also want You to use me to reach other people. Ooo, the possibilities are endless! Maybe I'll sing on the worship team. Serve in children's church. Hand out food at an outreach. Maybe I can visit the shut-ins or take meals to the homeless. Maybe I can share a scripture in Sunday school or help my teacher clean up the room afterward.

Yep, I love my church. I love my friends—old and new—and love the adults too. It's a great place to hang out. Best of all, Lord, it's an amazing place to worship You! When I go to church, I can stand with other Christians and sing songs of praise. That makes me the happiest of all! Amen.

You should not stay away from the church meetings, as some are doing, but you should meet together and encourage each other. Do this even more as you see the day coming.
HEBREWS 10:25 NCV

Inner Beauty

I like to look pretty, Lord. I like to get dressed up, fix my hair, and feel like a princess. But no matter how hard I try, there's always someone I think is prettier than me.

Whether it's someone at school who has better hair or cuter clothes, or the images I see on television and on the Internet, it seems like I'll never measure up. It just doesn't seem fair, Lord, that some girls got all the breaks in the looks department, and I didn't.

But when I really think about it, the thing that draws me to others isn't the way they look or how they dress. The thing that makes me want to spend time with someone is their personality. How do they treat me? How do they make me feel about myself when I'm around them?

I guess that's what You call inner beauty. And if it's what draws me to other people, I'll bet that's what will draw others to me. Lord, help me to spend more time on my inner beauty—on making others feel loved, accepted, and important—than on what I look like on the outside. Amen.

Let your adorning be the hidden person of the
heart with the imperishable beauty of
a gentle and quiet spirit.
1 PETER 3:4 ESV

My Parents

I want my parents to be proud of me, Lord. I want to make them happy, make them smile, make them glad that I'm their daughter. But sometimes it's hard...like when they don't see things the way I see them or they don't let me do the things I want to do.

I watch kids on television and even my friends at school treating their parents with disrespect. Rebellion is viewed as cool, and parents are seen as backward and nerdy.

But I know that's not right. My parents may not be perfect, but they love me more than anyone else in this world, besides You, God. They want what's best for me. Even when I don't agree with their decisions, I know their choices for me are ruled by that love.

Help me to honor them, Lord, with the way I treat them in person and the way I act when they're not around. I want them to know they can trust me. I want them to know I'll do the right thing, out of respect for them. In everything I do, I want to bring joy to their hearts—and to Yours. Amen.

A wise son brings joy to his father,
but a foolish son brings grief to his mother.
PROVERBS 10:1 NIV

Day 363
All Things Work
Together for Good

Lord, sometimes I just don't understand. Your Word says that all things work together for good. But this doesn't feel *good*. It feels *awful*. It seems like everything goes wrong for me. I know that I have many blessings, but I just don't understand why You let certain things happen. I am hurt by other people, even those whom I thought loved me. I am disappointed. I feel like I am missing out. Some days it seems like every other girl in the world is getting what I want while I am left empty-handed. At times, I feel all alone.

The Bible tells me to cast my cares on You because You care for me. I lay them at Your feet, God. Help me not to scramble to pick up my worries again but to leave them with You. You are big enough to handle all my hurts, disappointments, and confusion. Work all things together in my life, Father. Work them together for good. . .even when I do not understand. Amen.

And we know that in all things God works for
the good of those who love him, who have
been called according to his purpose.
ROMANS 8:28 NIV

Day 364
Hello? Is Anyone There?

I love staying busy, Father! There's so much to do, so many people to hang out with and fun things to enjoy. I love being on the go all the time. Life would be boring if I didn't have so much to do.

Sometimes I get so busy that I forget to spend time with You, and that's not good. I don't want You to have to come looking for me. I don't want You to have to say, "Hello? Is anyone there?" I want to be there every day, Your loving daughter, ready to spend time with You in Your Word and in prayer.

There's a lot of stuff on my calendar. I'm a busy girl! But there's nothing else I can possibly do that will be more important than spending time with my Daddy, God. The Bible is my personal invitation to spend time with You. Draw me close to You, Lord. May I never forget You, even on my busiest day! Amen.

Don't let the excitement of youth cause you to forget your Creator. Honor him in your youth before you grow old and say, "Life is not pleasant anymore."
ECCLESIASTES 12:1 NLT

Day 365
My Bedtime Prayer

Dear Father, thank You for this day. Once again, You have faithfully brought me through all that has happened to me since I woke up. You have met each of my needs— food, clothing, and shelter—and have blessed me even more beyond that. I have received the benefit of Your goodness.

I spent time with those I love, my family and friends. You have kept me safe and have given me a place to sleep. I can lie down, confident that You will be watching me all night long, because You never sleep. Nothing can happen to me that You do not allow.

Please help me to sleep well, and if I dream, may they be dreams that are good. You are my safe place, and I now fall asleep, fully entrusting my care to You.

Even now, prepare my day tomorrow. May I wake full of Your joy and face the day with a positive attitude. May I be a blessing to each person I come in contact with throughout the day. And may I commit to grow even closer to You as I continue my journey.

Good night, Father. Amen.

In peace I will lie down and sleep, for you alone,
LORD, make me dwell in safety.
PSALM 4:8 NIV

Contributor Index

Emily Biggers is a Tennessee native living in Arlington, Texas. She loves to travel, write, spend time with family and friends, and decorate.

Renae Brumbaugh is a freelance writer, author, syndicated newspaper columnist, teacher, and mom. In her free time, she leaps tall buildings in a single bound and rescues kittens out of trees. Or at least she might try to do those things if she had free time....

Jennifer Hahn is a freelance writer, editor, and proofreader. She lives in Pennsylvania's Amish country with her husband and three children.

Janice Hanna hails from south Texas. She is a Christian author and mother of four grown daughters. Janice has written more than forty books, most under the name Janice A. Thompson.
Janice's Readings: Days 20, 40, 42, 50, 51, 70, 71, 80, 90, 100, 108, 110, 120, 140, 150, 160, 170, 180, 190, 200, 210, 220, 230, 240, 250, 260, 268, 280, 290, 310, 320, 330, 340, 350, 360, 364

Missy Horsfall, a pastor's wife for more than twenty years, is a Bible study teacher, board member, and speaker for Circle of Friends Ministries.
Missy's Readings: Days 6, 16, 26, 36, 56, 66, 76, 85, 86, 94, 96, 103, 106, 126, 136, 146, 156, 158, 166, 186, 196, 226, 236, 246, 256, 266, 286, 293, 296, 316, 326, 336, 337, 346, 356

Tina Krause is a freelance writer, editor, and award-winning newspaper columnist in Valparaiso, Indiana. She and her husband, Jim, have five grandchildren.
Tina's Readings: Days 17, 27, 37, 47, 57, 62, 67, 77, 87, 97, 101, 107, 117, 118, 127, 137, 147, 167, 177, 187, 197, 207, 217, 227, 237, 247, 257, 267, 283, 287, 297, 307, 317, 327, 347, 357

Donna Maltese is a freelance writer, editor, and proofreader as well as a pastor's prayer partner. She lives in Pennsylvania with her family.

Donna's Readings: Days 4, 8, 14, 34, 46, 74, 84, 91, 98, 104, 124, 125, 144, 154, 164, 174, 184, 194, 201, 204, 214, 222, 234, 235, 244, 245, 254, 270, 284, 294, 303, 304, 314, 324, 328, 334, 344

Prayers by Donna Maltese were inspired by the following girls, ages 10 to 14, from three different families—Kendall, Madalynne, and Hannah Geib; Grace and Lizzie Hogue; Sydni and Savannah Stockert.

Kelly McIntosh is a full-time editorial director. She and her husband, John, live in Ohio with their twin son and daughter.

Kelly's Readings: Days 143, 223, 322

Brigitta Nortker takes every opportunity to travel that she can. In her free time, she enjoys an excellent book, a cup of coffee, and spending time with friends and family.

Brigitta's Readings: Days 1, 10, 11, 21, 30, 31, 41, 44, 52, 60, 61, 81, 111, 121, 131, 134, 151, 157, 161, 171, 181, 191, 192, 211, 221, 231, 241, 251, 261, 271, 291, 301, 311, 321, 331, 341, 351

MariLee Parrish lives in Ohio with her husband, Eric, and young children. She's a freelance musician and writer who desires to paint a picture of God with her life, talents, and ministries.

MariLee's Readings: Days 7, 18, 24, 28, 38, 48, 49, 58, 78, 114, 116, 128, 130, 138, 168, 178, 188, 198, 208, 218, 228, 238, 248, 258, 275, 276, 278, 288, 298, 300, 308, 318, 338, 348, 354, 358

Valorie Quesenberry is a pastor's wife, mother, musician, editor of a Christian ladies' magazine, and writer. She periodically contributes devotionals to a Christian literature provider.

Valorie's Readings: Days 3, 13, 15, 22, 23, 43, 63, 64, 73, 83, 93, 123, 142, 153, 163, 173, 176, 183, 193, 213, 232, 233, 243, 253, 263, 273, 306, 323, 343, 349, 353

Scripture Index

More Books for Girls!

Choose Extraordinary

Be encouraged to live an extraordinary life for God with these 180 devotions and prayers. Each reading will challenge you to be courageous in your faith like dozens of Bible heroines including Esther, Hannah, Mary, Ruth, the Woman Who Needed Healing, and more! Be captured by truth, adventure, and Bible heroines galore!

Paperback / 978-1-64352-803-8 / $4.99

Dare to Be a Courageous Girl

This delightfully unique journal will challenge you to live boldly for God! With each turn of the page, you will encounter a new "dare" from the easy-to-understand New Life Version of scripture alongside a brief devotional reading and thought-provoking journal prompt or "challenge" that encourages you to take action and obey God's Word.

Paperback / 978-1-64352-642-3 / $14.99